Building the Data-Driven Law Firm
Second Edition

EDITED BY ALEX DAVIES

Commissioning editor
Alex Davies

Managing director
Sian O'Neill

Building the Data-Driven Law Firm, second edition
is published by

Globe Law and Business Ltd
3 Mylor Close
Horsell
Woking
Surrey GU21 4DD
United Kingdom
Tel: +44 20 3745 4770
www.globelawandbusiness.com

Building the Data-Driven Law Firm, second edition

ISBN 978-1-78742-922-2
EPUB ISBN 978-1-78742-923-9
Adobe PDF ISBN 978-1-78742-924-6

© 2022 Globe Law and Business Ltd except where otherwise indicated.

The right of the contributors to be identified as authors of this work has been asserted by them in accordance with sections 77 and 78 of the Copyright, Designs and Patents Act 1988.

All rights reserved. No part of this publication may be reproduced in any material form (including photocopying, storing in any medium by electronic means or transmitting) without the written permission of the copyright owner, except in accordance with the provisions of the Copyright, Designs and Patents Act 1988 or under terms of a licence issued by the Copyright Licensing Agency Ltd, 5th Floor, Shackleton House, 4 Battle Bridge Lane, London SE1 2HX, United Kingdom (www.cla.co.uk, email: licence@cla.co.uk). Applications for the copyright owner's written permission to reproduce any part of this publication should be addressed to the publisher.

DISCLAIMER
This publication is intended as a general guide only. The information and opinions which it contains are not intended to be a comprehensive study, or to provide legal advice, and should not be treated as a substitute for legal advice concerning particular situations. Legal advice should always be sought before taking any action based on the information provided. The publisher bears no responsibility for any errors or omissions contained herein.

Contents

Executive summary vii

About the authors xi

Chapter 1: A single source of truth for your firm
By David Curle, legal content and research lead, Litera
    Introduction 1
    Removing barriers that separate data into silos 1
    A single source of truth for strategic planning 2
    A single source of truth for marketing and business development 3
    Data in marketing strategy and communications 4
    Data in biography content management 5
    A single source of truth for winning more business –
    pricing and scoping 5
    A single source of truth for service delivery excellence 6
    Experience management for staffing 6
    Collaboration – identifying and addressing white space 7
    Legal project management 8
    A single source of truth as the engine for strategic growth 9

Chapter 2: Unlocking contractual data
By Shilpa Bhandarkar and Doug Donahue, Linklaters | CreateiQ
    Defining "contractual" data and appreciating its potential 11
    Accessibility of contractual data and the need for
    "structured" data 12
    What digital platforms and structured data enable us to do 14
    What this looks like in practice: Derivatives industry
    case study – ISDA Create 16
    What does this mean for law firms? 18

Contents

Chapter 3: Law firms' approach to talent and the current lack of data collection
By Phil Burdon and Tom Spence, Donoma Advisors

- Introduction 21
- What areas of data are currently used in the industry? 22
- Is there greater potential to use people data? 24
- Desire for change exists 25
- Challenges for change 25
- Critical factors for success 28
- Conclusion 29

Chapter 4: Data Bites
By Joanne Frears, solicitor, Lionshead Law

- Definitions and interpretation 31
- Big Data 32
- Big Data, smart data, and value-add 34
- Data, trust, and confidence in the profession 36
- Outliers 40

Chapter 5: Data in a remote environment
By Silvia Bauer, Luther Rechtsanwaltsgesellschaft mbH

- Introduction 43
- General data protection requirements 44
- Regulations for technical-organizational measures for mobile working 47
- Data exchange 50
- Control rights for mobile working 51
- Conclusion 52

Chapter 6: Building a data-driven business development strategy
By Yolanda Cartusciello, PP&C Consulting

- Learnings from data: people say one thing and do another 55
- Bringing data into content marketing 56
- Using data to inform business development 58
- Using data to inform the "go/no go process" 60
- Using data to improve proposals and interviews 61
- Using data to improve service delivery 62
- The new data frontier 63

Chapter 7: Analyzing data to increase efficiencies – the client's perspective
By Mori Kabiri, InfiniGlobe LLC

- What are metrics, KPIs, and KRIs? 65
- What's the report on reports? 67
- Where to source the freshest data 68
- Financial reports that make cents (sense) 69
- Operations analysis and results 71
- More advanced invoice data analytics 76

Chapter 8: Why your data might be useless
By Jaap Bosman, consultant – partner

- Snake oil 79
- Data, an early experience 80
- 25 percent savings on external legal spend 81
- CRM frustrations 82
- Financial analysis – risks and shortcomings 83
- Much of the data is "useless" 84
- Data analysis for law firms 85
- Prediction and prevention 86
- Data are the alpha and the omega 86

Chapter 9: Data in the 2020s
By Paul Brook, Dell Technologies

- Data at the top table 90
- Hot or not? 93
- Threats and opportunities 96
- Summary 101

About Globe Law and Business 103

Executive summary

Like so many other professions, law is becoming increasingly influenced by an overwhelming amount of disparate, fragmented, and complex data that can both help and hinder business. Data comes from a wealth of different sources, both internal and external, constantly changing, never still. Keeping control of all that data is one challenge; leveraging it to the greater good much harder.

Despite the huge amount of data in the average law firm, data-driven decision-making is relatively new and uncharted. With the hugely disruptive changes that have occurred in our ways of working over the last two years, the issue of data is now front and centre.

This second edition of *Building the Data-Driven Law Firm* looks at how the use of data has become inextricably linked with the practice of law; how it can be utilized to the good, and the safeguards that must be put in place to mitigate the bad; how Big Data will revolutionize the way lawyers work, and the cases they will work on; and how new uses for data will influence the law firm of the future. Bringing the book bang up to date, new content features how we can keep data secure in the changing world of work, how data can be used for business development and client satisfaction, the implications of data bias and data theft, and whether the way we use data is even useful anymore.

In many firms, data is locked away in information systems that often operate independently from each other. There is great value in those data sets, but law firms often lack the resources, skill, and infrastructure to bring them together under a data strategy that delivers better outcomes for clients. Becoming a data-driven organization is not a single event or even a series of tactical steps. It's more of a mindset or a strategic approach to how a firm handles its data. At Litera, explains David Curle, author of chapter one, this approach is known as "a single source of truth", because its ultimate goal is to ensure that all available data support every decision and that people in the firm can rely on that data as the most current, accurate basis for those decisions. This chapter offers guidance on how firms can start to derive more value from the data that they already have, in their marketing, planning, billing, matter management, experience management, and pricing and budgeting systems.

In chapter two, Shilpa Bhandarkar and Doug Donahue of Linklaters | CreateiQ look at how contracts, and the process of creating and negotiating them, represent the most abundant and valuable form of legal and audit data. However, businesses can rarely access or manipulate this data in its current form – linguistic data buried in MS Word and PDF documents. Through the process of standardization and thoughtful digitization, they argue, lawyers can start to capture structured and machine-readable contractual data that can then be exploited by AI technologies and form the basis for true automation. These "full-stack" lawyers will be able to provide an entirely different experience and level of service to their clients, partnering with them to unlock valuable business intelligence, spot trends, and proactively prevent issues from arising, all underpinned by accurate and current contractual data.

Chapter three then looks to assess the increasing use of data when assessing law firms' approach to talent. Even today, the only datasets used across the industry to track the ultimate success or failure of a lawyer have been recording a combination of billable hours and associated revenues and profits. Increasingly however, HR and leadership figures are considering how to bring the use of data into more areas of talent management and linking this to different targets and indeed compensation structures for fee-earners. There is also a further opportunity to bring the use of data into external talent strategies with the aim of increasing the success rate of lawyers who are brought into the firm as lateral hires. This chapter by Phil Burdon and Tom Spence of Donoma Advisors explores possible ways in which data can play a role in helping law firms identify, attract, retain, and reward fee earners through an increase in the use of data.

In chapter four, Joanne Frears, solicitor at Lionshead Law, analyses a number of issues pertinent to the use of data today. Using data provides the "value add" that lawyers increasingly seek to differentiate their practice from another firms. She asks, if a law firm owns that data, what trends and indices can it safely and sagely provide as "advice" or "information" to clients?

When client confidentiality remains at the heart of professional practice worldwide, this chapter considers how data can be interrogated and used whilst maintaining secrecy and privilege. If trust in the legal profession is low, will having access to data help rebuild trust and confidence in the profession or not? Or do the ethical issues of data bias make all Big Data fundamentally flawed and potentially unethical and thus intrinsically unhelpful for lawyers? In every industry there are "outliers" and she poses the question, what if that's the data your client really needs? How can lawyers use the minority reports and outliers and provide those to their clients without risk? Joanna touches on data sovereignty and indemnity matters and considers if insurance and indemnities offer adequate protection when data bites back?

Even before the COVID-19 pandemic broke out, remote work was becoming more and more attractive – both for employees who benefit from more flexible working hours, time and cost savings, but also for companies who save on rent, ancillary costs and benefit from more satisfied employees. New circumstances demand new standards – also with regard to data protection and security. Even if employees work remotely, the employer as data controller has to comply with the requirements of the relevant data protection laws – in the EU, and for those countries dealing with EU-based companies, this is the General Data Protection Regulation (GDPR).

Even in the remote office, personal data must be protected against unauthorized access, improper destruction, insecure transmission, and similar traps that can lead to a data breach. In addition to appropriate and suitable hardware and software, and the implementation of adequate technical measures, organizational measures such as guidelines and training, which both inform and oblige employees, is indispensable. Chapter six, by Silvia Bauer, Luther Rechtsanwaltsgesellschaft mbH, describes what measures a company must implement to ensure compliance with applicable data protection law, especially the General Data Protection Regulation (GDPR), when employees work remotely. Data breaches can not only undermine client confidence in the company but can lead to expensive fines. To ensure compliance includes implementation of organizational measures such as remote working policies and cybersecurity policies. This chapter summarizes how personal data can be adequately protected in the remote office.

Moving away from the risks posed by data, chapter six by Yolanda Cartusciello, PP&C Consulting, examines real case studies and examples of how firms are using data to drive business development strategies and decisions. Yolanda looks at how data can inform our content marketing efforts, plan our business development activities, improve our "go/no go" process, shape our proposals and interviews, and improve service delivery. The chapter looks at how to begin the process of collecting and analyzing meaningful data for the benefit of the firm.

Following this, chapter seven, by Mori Kabiri of InfiniGlobe LLC, and an entrepreneur with two decades of designing technology for the legal industry, reviews some of the methods, metrics, and KPIs used by corporate legal departments to evaluate firms' performances. Mori's chapter provides an overview of two decades working with US and EU corporations to analyze law firm ebilling data and how this has helped improve performance.

It is often said that data is the new gold. Even a term like "data mining" seems to suggest that there are riches that one just has to unearth. Reality, surprisingly, could not be more different. Most data is absolutely useless to serve as a basis for meaningful analysis. Chapter eight, by Jaap Bosman, consultant – partner at TGO Consulting, explains in easy-to-understand practical terms what standards a usable dataset must meet. Not only does the data need to be clean, it also needs to be complete and unbiased. All this is much harder than it seems and requires considerable efforts and funding. The legal industry came late to the game in terms of the use of data and data analytics. Today there is a cottage industry offering data-related services to the sector. Law firms, struck by data fever and fearing to miss out on essential developments, has jumped on the bandwagon. Unsurprisingly, the number of success stories remains underwhelming. This chapter, therefore, highlights the economic aspects of data gathering and analysis. Under what conditions will the process deliver a return on the investment? In other words: how, if at all, can data make you money?

The 2020s will be defined by data. Global companies and household names such as Apple, Amazon, Meta (Facebook), and Google are all creating and consuming huge volumes of data whilst at the same time turning it into viable business outcomes. Data is being used to drive efficiencies in business and in governments; it is being curated into scientific and artistic discovery, new knowledge and intellectual property; data is being turned into money. The Data Decade is likely to have a profound impact upon the legal world. Questions will abound, answers will be scarce. Do you need a digital twin to operate within the virtual world? What *is* a digital twin? Will artificial intelligence replace human expertise? Should the legal profession use AI to enhance customer service, to generate new revenue streams? This final chapter, by Paul Brook of Dell Technologies, challenges thinking, leads with examples, and intends to leave you with more questions than answers. But asking the right question is often the best place to start.

About the authors

Silvia C. Bauer is a lawyer and partner at Luther Rechtsanwaltsgesellschaft mbH. She specializes in assistance pertaining to data privacy and information technology. Among other things, she conducts data privacy audits and advises national and international companies on the organization of their data protection and the safeguarding of data protection compliance worldwide. Furthermore, Silvia acts as data protection officer for various national and international companies and company groups. She is a guest lecturer at numerous events related to data protection and IT law and regularly publishes articles regarding data protection issues in various journals.

Shilpa Bhandarkar is the CEO of CreateiQ, Linklaters' proprietary CLM platform. CreateiQ takes a data-first approach to contracting, making the process of drafting, negotiating, and executing contracts faster, smarter, and more accurate, while simultaneously giving users real-time access to structured contractual and audit data. Over 240 institutions are using CreateiQ, including some of the world's largest banks and investment managers. Shilpa started her career as a project finance lawyer but her interest in technology and entrepreneurship led her to found, build, and sell a mobile app company as well as grow a LegalTech start-up through a Series A before re-joining Linklaters in 2018 as its global head of innovation. She sits on the firm's innovation steering group, which is responsible for the firm's strategic approach to innovation and efficiency. Shilpa was listed as a leading "Disruptor" in The Lawyer Hot 100, 2019 and an "Individual winner" of the "TechWomen100 Awards 2018".

Jaap Bosman is an award-winning strategy consultant and an investor. After having spent 15 years in legal practice, he founded TGO Consulting, a highly successful consulting boutique that works with elite law firms and premier legal departments throughout the world. His achievements have been recognized in 2013 by the *Financial Times* with the first ever Innovative Lawyers Award for International Strategy. He is also a winner of the Thomson Reuters Excellence in Legal Marketing Award. Jaap has published three books and he regularly contributes articles to Bloomberg, the ABA Journal, the ACC Docket, and various other leading publications around the world. Jaap is a seasoned consultant and widely considered one of the world's most influential thought leaders on the business of law.

Paul Brook works for Dell Technologies as pre-sales director for data-centric workloads in the Europe, Middle East, and Africa (EMEA) region. His team works with customers, business partners, and technology integrators across EMEA, describing and designing platforms that help to make money and save money for businesses and public sector organizations as part of their data-driven digital transformation. Author of two books, *The Life of AI* and *The Shape of Data*, Paul has held several roles at Dell Technologies from CTO to Cloud program manager. Prior to Dell, Paul worked in the applications development and managed services sectors. Before joining the IT industry, he worked for a consultancy that specialized in business performance improvement.

Phil Burdon has been an advisor to the legal services market for over 15 years and has co-founded two talent advisory firms. He enjoys advising international and domestic law firms on their key strategic priorities and placing senior in-house lawyers into financial institutions. He spends his time developing and executing projects of strategic importance to clients who have often been very long standing. A chartered management consultant and a member of the Institute of Consulting (CMI), Phil is well informed on the cross-border legal services landscape, domestic and international talent markets, as well as the changing demands clients place on their instructed law firms.

For more than 20 years, **Yolanda Cartusciello** has served in senior administrative leadership roles in major law firms, including Debevoise & Plimpton and Cleary Gottlieb. She has led marketing teams, designed business development and media strategies, and implemented client development programs. She has been the chief architect of profile enhancement strategies, perception studies, branding exercises, comprehensive client interview programs, and practice and lateral partner rollouts. She has adapted the customer journey mapping technique for use by law firms and has trained and advised firms on its use. Yolanda is a self-described "data nerd" and has worked with numerous firms on establishing a protocol for collecting meaningful data and employing it to help firms develop data-driven marketing and business development strategies.

David Curle is legal content and research lead at Litera, a legal technology provider with a platform of integrated offerings that support law firms with document workflow, collaboration, and data management. He came to Litera with its acquisition of Kira Systems, which provides a machine learning-based platform for analyzing legal documents such as contracts. Prior to Kira, he supported the Thomson Reuters Institute with content and analysis of the role of technology in the transformation of the legal industry. He has a JD from the University of Minnesota Law School.

Doug Donahue is a finance partner in Linklaters' New York office and a CreateiQ Board member. He represents some of the firm's foremost clients – ranging from banks to hedge funds – on a wide variety of financial products. Doug has a long-standing and deep interest in legal technology. He advised ISDA and IHS Markit on the creation, design, and development of ISDA Amend (a joint-venture online platform that has transformed the ISDA protocol process and has over 100,000 users). He also led Linklaters' collaboration with ISDA on the development of ISDA Create. ISDA Create is a digital negotiation platform that allows market participants to create, negotiate, and execute ISDA documentation completely online, revolutionizing the way in which market participants put in place their derivatives documentation. In his role as a board member of CreateiQ (the wider CLM platform that powers ISDA Create), Doug leads Linklaters' efforts to build, leverage, and adapt legal technology to enhance the delivery of legal services.

Joanne Frears works at Lionshead Law, a firm that has been an entirely digital practice for ten years. She works on complex contracts and advising clients on protecting their innovative technology. One of the first women solicitors in the City to specialize in advising businesses on IT law, Joanne has been through many business cycles with her clients since she qualified in the mid-1990s and seen numerous technologies lauded as the "next big thing". From this perspective she considers the future of law, statute, and the legal profession. Joanne has written numerous publications on law and technology and business development for lawyers. She is a visiting professor at Aston University and a visiting professional at Reading University and the Worshipful Company of Goldsmiths. She is a member of the IBA and holds a Masters in comparative EU, UK, and US IP law.

Mori Kabiri, of InfiniGlobe LLC, is a thought leader and innovator in software automation solutions and professional services for corporate legal departments and law firms. Mori has worked throughout the legal industry over the last 25+ years, holding management roles in leading legal technology vendors, corporate legal departments, and management consulting firms, and is a member of Forbes council and entrepreneur with two legal technology start-ups under his belt. He has a progressive track record in forging innovative technology solutions for many Fortune 500 companies dealing with complex processes and regulations across the world. While leading InfiniGlobe, Mori has engaged the academic community and co-authored a scientific paper exploring the benefits of training machine learning on law firm invoice data, published and presented at ICDM 2021, for which he was also asked to be a conference chair. His articles in legal technology trends have been published in Forbes and Mori has a long-established relationship with the University of California, providing mentorship for technology and law students.

Tom Spence is the co-founder of Donoma Advisors, an advisory firm within the legal sector that works with law firm leaders on their market and talent strategies internationally. Tom is a chartered and certified management consultant and sits on the UK Institute of Consulting's National Advisory Committee as well as the Institute of Consulting's London and South East Committee. In recent years, Tom has contributed to a number of publications on how the legal industry can improve people processes and investments.

Chapter 1:
How law firms leverage data for superior client experience and growth

By David Curle, legal content and research lead, Litera

Introduction

Businesses of all kinds leverage data as an asset for finding customers, increasing revenues and profits, and more effectively competing against others. Virtually every industry has been transformed by the availability of data and by the ability to leverage data to support better business decisions.

Law firms are no different from other businesses in this regard. Firms that leverage their data as a strategic differentiator in an increasingly competitive landscape will capture a more significant share of the market, operate at higher efficiency, and deliver greater value to their clients. Accurate data, and the proper analysis of that data, can guide firms toward better decisions. However, data collection and analysis are not simple tasks. Many firms do not have access to data scientists or analysts who can make sense of the data they possess – but those skills are in demand.

So how does a firm know what data to collect? And how can it create a data strategy across all the different moving parts that make up the modern law firm?

Becoming a data-driven organization is not a single event or even a series of tactical steps. It's more of a mindset or a strategic approach to how a firm handles its data. We call this approach "A Single Source of Truth" because its ultimate goal is to ensure that all available data support every decision and that people in the firm can rely on that data as the most current, accurate basis for those decisions.

Removing barriers that separate data into silos

In a recent webinar during Litera's recent Changing Lawyer Summit,[1] the director of knowledge management at a large US law firm put the problem succinctly: *"Lawyers want one place to go for the answer. The answers have to be definitive."*

The statement can be taken a step further: all professionals in a law firm – whether they work as lawyers or in marketing, business development, finance, or other operational roles – want that single source for definitive answers. The problem, she noted, is that the data a lawyer might need for a given task tends to be held in separate systems – financial and billing systems, document management systems, client/matter lookup systems, client relationship management (CRM) systems, marketing systems, knowledge management systems. Data in all those legacy systems is a by-product of many separate processes. Today's challenge is to normalize and integrate all that data because lawyers and firm management ask questions that often require data from more than one system.

Law firms are only recently starting to catch up with other industries in figuring out how to get data from those systems to work together. In that same Summit conversation, the same firm's director of analytics pointed out that removing those barriers and harmonizing data is a matter of data governance. Controlling how data is generated and standardizing practices across all of a firm's systems is the key. "What one of us knows, all of us have to know."

This practice of good data governance needs to engage the entire firm – by its very nature, it requires multidisciplinary solutions, with expertise coming from lawyers, technologists, operational staff, and business experts.

So, broadly speaking, that problem of creating a single source of truth permeates many different functions in today's law firms. This chapter addresses some specific ways firm leaders address the challenges across various systems and functions to help firms gain a competitive edge in strategic planning, marketing and business development, pricing and scoping matters, and service delivery.

A single source of truth for strategic planning
Even before a firm's lawyers can provide superior legal services, a firm's management needs a strategy that maps out the firm's direction and guides the specific actions and key performance indicators for legal teams and individual lawyers.

Many firms are very good at understanding their clients and markets, but many fail at execution. A brilliant plan is wasted if it sits in a drawer or an online folder and never comes to life in the day-to-day decisions made by individuals in the firm. Moving those strategic plans to the right software platform will embed the plans into lawyers' workflows across the firm.

Dr Heidi Gardner, distinguished fellow at Harvard Law School and head of a research and advisory firm, has documented this "strategy to execution gap" in her research.[2] She notes that this challenge is not limited to law firms. Across all industries, 57 percent of senior executives in an Economist survey[3] found that their strategy implementations were unsuccessful.

In the legal domain, Gardner[4] has found that "smart" collaboration that engages the collective knowledge and experience of the entire firm is critical. But while 70 percent of firms embrace collaboration as a core pillar of their plans, the collaboration seems to break down in the execution phases.

Gardner identifies three imperatives that can help a firm break down those barriers to collaborative execution of strategic plans:

- *Clarity of strategic direction* – individuals need to understand the rationale behind the firm's strategies;
- *Discipline* – sometimes sticking to a strategy requires saying "no," or making sometimes counter-intuitive choices in support of a plan; and
- *Accountability* – successful strategic plans measure outcomes, flag potential trouble spots, and track and reward outcomes visibly.

Software is essential to support the execution of all three of those imperatives. Gardner recommends investing in industry-specific software that can capture everyone's responsibilities and tasks and make them transparent for the whole firm. Data and metrics captured from internal systems can be pushed through individualized dashboards and other tools that keep plans and outcomes front and center for everyone engaged in execution.

A single source of truth for marketing and business development

Law firms' marketing and business development departments are also starting to leverage data. Law is a knowledge-intensive industry; firms need to be able to communicate about the intangibles that differentiate their expertise and service delivery apart from other firms and engage clients in new ways.

Technology and data have revolutionized marketing, and law firm marketing and business development functions are becoming more professionalized. A recent survey[5] by recruiting firm Calibrate Legal found that the ratio of law firm partners to marketing and BD professionals was 12:1 in North America and 5:1 in the UK. That same study found that firm spending on sponsorships and in-person events is down (partly due to the COVID-19 pandemic). At the same time, a very high percentage of larger firms (89 percent) intend to increase digital marketing technology and program spending.

That shift from in-person to digital marketing requires a new orientation toward data.

Data in marketing strategy and communications

Law firm marketing is typically focused on content and events. That is appropriate in a knowledge-based industry where expertise is the product; establishing a firm's thought leadership and brand attributes and building trusted relationships are critical in that context. This is different from many other industries, which have marketing processes more focused on driving a more comprehensive range of potential customers through a lead generation funnel. The software supporting legal marketing teams needs to be responsive to that difference and support law firms' more significant emphasis on relationships and client engagement.

So what does a single source of truth for marketing and business development look like in legal?

On the business development side, it means that teams have a complete profile for each client (derived from data about billing, matters, behaviors, content, events, industries, and markets) in a single location. Having that data aggregated and at hand enables business development professionals to spend less time tracking down the data, and more time tailoring the conversations it wants to have and strengthening those relationships to win more business.

It means enabling and automating the marketing motions that get content into the right hands on the marketing side. Having access to customer data on any critical data point allows firms to personalize content and ensure scope relevance to grow engagement with it. Many marketers spend time on repetitive manual tasks – matching data between systems, exporting and importing lists, managing opt-outs, etc. A single source of truth eliminates all of this, giving them more time to spend on activities that can move the needle, such as developing strategies, producing content, and testing various approaches.

Today's firms can do so much more to tell their stories in terms that potential clients will respond to. And the most significant difference between yesterday's firm and today's is the availability of data that can tell that story.

Software tailored to the marketing needs of law firms supports that work in two ways. First, bringing critical data together provides the most accurate view of clients and enables marketing and business development teams to develop strategies to drive engagement and brand. Second, software can automate many of the motions it takes to deliver content and marketing messages, conserving resources for the higher value work of thought leadership and relationship building.

Data in biography content management
Despite the new technology-enabled marketing capabilities that firms now enjoy, the firm's greatest asset is still the expertise of its lawyers. The lawyer biography is still one of the most valuable marketing tools available. Traditional lawyer bios have been seen as relatively static, text-based pieces of content. At best, firms maintained current bios with a manual update and cut-and-paste as needed for various uses.

Many firms are turning to software to leverage lawyer bios into a much more dynamic and flexible marketing asset, something much easier to maintain and distribute than with manual methods. According to a recent ILTA Marketing Technologies Survey,[6] about 30 percent of firms are actively seeking to acquire new experience management technology.

The best of these systems pull data from multiple sources across a firm and integrate it with key applications. Biographical data can be combined with key experience data from billing and matter systems, and updated data from those sources can be automatically pushed to websites. Once linked together, all that data can easily flow into firm-branded pitches, proposals, and submissions of various kinds, where the firm's expertise can be highlighted. Finally, the aggregated bio and profile data can be used to efficiently search the firm for specific experience and knowledge in preparation for pitches and RFPs. With a single source of truth about their lawyers' collective expertise, law firms can spend less time chasing down biographical data, credentials, publications, and the like and more time leveraging that material to build client relationships through tailored communications and proposals.

A single source of truth for winning more business – pricing and scoping
Increasingly, potential clients expect that pitches and responses to requests for proposals include accurate pricing, scoping, and staffing. Achieving the level of accuracy and predictability that clients expect requires data pulled from multiple sources.

In a recent Altman Weil Law Firms in Transition survey,[7] 91.5 percent of respondents believed that "more price competition" among firms was a permanent trend. In an era when clients are increasingly looking for more transparent, predictable pricing, and when fixed fees for certain services are in demand, data-supported pricing processes are essential. Pricing and budgeting without robust supporting data is a recipe for write-offs and disappointed clients.

The cornerstone of a system for accurate budgeting that wins new business and builds loyal clients is a matter management platform that answers the critical questions – who does what, when, where, and at what cost.

The challenge here is to meet client requests for legal work with accurate data from multiple sources. Matter management platforms that capture the time and rates used in past matters, plus precise measures of the profitability of those matters, are the core elements of any pricing response. But the accuracy of fee-setting will also depend on the firm's ability to understand which past matters were genuinely similar to the work proposed. That accuracy is dependent on the firm's ability to capture the exact types of activity that have gone into past matters; the time spent on each step, the seniority level, and cost of the lawyers and other professionals working on them.

Ultimately, pricing and scoping lie at the intersection of the client's needs and expectations and the firm's resources and capabilities. Having software that unifies this data, makes sense of it, and surfaces it in real-time to whoever needs it within the firm, eliminates the needlessly burdensome process of reaching out to multiple data sources within the firm. Having data to support accurate, predictable prices and budgets is a long-term play that helps cement client loyalty and adds to a firm's competitive strengths.

A single source of truth for service delivery excellence

Once the work is won and the budget set, the focus turns to execution – deploying lawyers with the best-matched experience and expertise profiles and delivering work on time, within budget, and within scope. Ideally, well-planned implementation will reduce write-downs and write-offs and improve client transparency. Three broad types of software tools are helping law firms improve their execution:

- Experience management tools;
- Collaboration tools; and
- Legal project management tools.

Experience management for staffing

Good data on past matters is not just important for pricing legal work. It's essential to the efficient and optimal employment of a firm's human resources at its disposal. It's also necessary to staffing discussions with clients. In Altman Weil's Law Firms in Transitions study,[8] 72.5 percent of firms report "conversations about project staffing" as a key strategy for understanding client needs. An experience management system provides factual data to support decisions around talent and staffing in those conversations.

Experience management helps firms identify not just the "what?" and "how much?" components of a project proposal, but also the "who?" Knowing who has successfully worked on specific matters is an essential component of a data-driven approach to optimally staffing new matters. In the past, a partner's instincts, relationships, and anecdotal experience might have been the best basis for choosing the team to work on new matters. Now, firm data can be tapped to identify expertise in areas of law, practice-specific skills, bar admissions, and languages, and rich user profiles can track the relevant skills and expertise for each lawyer – but even when better data to support those decisions is available, pulling it all together can require a lot of effort from legal teams.

Firms can ensure that experience profiles are accurate and up to date with built-in approval processes and control with the right software platform. But software goes even beyond aggregating and standardizing lawyer profiles and expertise data; with the right industry-specific software, built-in intelligence can surface the profiles of the most appropriate people to work on a matter or even recommend the best team given the project's parameters.

Collaboration – identifying and addressing white space
As noted in the first section of this chapter, collaboration is key to setting and executing strategic plans. But collaboration across the firm on serving specific clients is another key success factor. Gardner's research is again relevant here. It shows that collaboration is increasingly important in a world where complex legal matters require law firms to respond with lawyer resources from more than one practice group. Law firms can measure the revenue effect of that collaboration by grouping and examining the average revenues received from clients served by similar numbers of practice groups. In one firm, she found that revenues from clients served by three practice groups were 5.7 times higher than the revenues from clients served by only one practice group. For clients served by five practice groups within the firm, revenues were 17.6 times higher than those served by only one practice group.

That's the multiplier effect of better collaboration – but how do firms get there? Technology and access to good data are essential. And there are signs that firms are investing more in collaboration, especially since the onset of the COVID-19 pandemic.

In a pair of surveys in 2020, the Bloomberg Law Legal Operations Survey and the Bloomberg Law Legal Tech Survey,[9] the number of law firms found to have implemented software-based collaboration tools jumped from 27 percent to 44 percent in just a few months between the surveys in March and July 2020.

How might technology enable more collaboration across the firm? First, law firms can create a central platform to manage firm, sector, practice, and client plans. But the platform must be designed for transparently sharing plans across the business, allowing individuals to align their objectives, and enabling easy collaboration among colleagues.

Second, firms can use data to identify clients being served by fewer practice groups than the firm's expertise could deliver – this is the "white space" opportunity that Gardner's research identified. A single source of truth approach, which proactively monitors client and matter data, analyses it, and highlights the opportunities to focus on, can keep firms ahead of those opportunities and enable them to reach out and cross-sell to the right clients. A software-based approach replaces the manual process of collecting that kind of data and turns a reactive process into a proactive one.

Legal project management
The sheer number of moving parts in a modern law firm makes it challenging to scale operations and project management. Keeping track of multiple matters, involving several departments across a host of timekeepers, is a herculean task.

Legal project management (LPM) tools have a double benefit for law firms. First, they provide a platform that helps lawyers plan and execute their work efficiently. Second, the very process of putting all that activity into a single platform also gives the firm valuable, standardized data on each project – data about timelines, costs, and labor inputs. That data, in turn, becomes the fodder for additional analysis and planning for future matters.

There is room for improvement in the profession's use of legal process management techniques and tools and opportunities for firms that apply them to differentiate themselves from the pack. The 2020 Altman Weil Law Firms in Transition survey shows that just 31.3 percent are providing ongoing project management training and support, and only 15.7 percent of firms have a full-time director of project management. But the opportunity is there; of the firms investing in LPM, 46.9 percent are experiencing "significant performance improvement".

LPM is also creating new career paths for lawyers and other professionals in law firms. LPM managers and data analysts have different skill sets than traditional lawyers. Many firms are finding lawyers eager to reorient their careers around these new skills, in many cases with the goal of a better work–life balance. The use of LPM and legal technology, in general, makes lives easier for lawyers by automating many tedious aspects of legal work, leaving time for more challenging and interesting client-facing work. Those work–life balance tradeoffs are increasingly important when recruiting and retaining lawyers, which is a real challenge for many firms.

A single source of truth as the engine for strategic growth

The examples above show that law firms sit on top of a large amount of valuable data that can be leveraged across many firm practices, functions, and processes. It should also be clear that data is often spread across a dizzying array of systems in many firms. In building up their technology stack, many firms have added layer upon layer of important systems – financial and billing systems, strategic planning applications, expertise databases, document management systems, matter and client systems, CRM systems, and various digital marketing tools.

Those systems were put in place for good reasons and perhaps yielded excellent results. But how to get to the next level? Software helps some of the most successful firms to bring the data in those systems together in a manner where the whole becomes more significant than the sum of the parts.

Every organization leverages data for strategic planning, targeting new business and marketing the firm, pricing and scoping work, and project managing its work. Law firms are not unique in needing data to optimize all those processes, but there are unique ways that firms operate and maintain their single source of truth. Software is the key to automating many of those processes that are often manual and labor-intensive today; industry-specific software gives law firms an extra edge by being responsive to the specific demands of legal service delivery.

References
1   www.litera.com/blog/top-5-takeaways-from-the-changing-lawyer-summit-2021/
2   Closing the 'Strategy to Execution' Gap, https://info.litera.com/closing-strategy-execution-gap-wp.html

3. Strategy execution: Achieving operational excellence, Economist Intelligence unit. http://graphics.eiu.com/files/ad_pdfs/celeran_eiu_wp.pdf
4. Heidi Gardner, "Implementing a Smart Collaboration Strategy, Part 1: Building the Case for Change." https://clp.law.harvard.edu/assets/Gardner-Matviak_Implementing-a-Smart-Collab-Strategy_Part-1.pdf
5. Law Firm Marketing/BD Department Size Study 2020, https://calibrate-strategies.com/marketing-bd-survey-2020/
6. ILTA Marketing Technology Survey, http://epubs.iltanet.org/i/1181316-mt19/0
7. Altman Weil, Law Firms in Transition 2020, https://altmanweil.com/wp-content/uploads/2022/06/Law-Firms-in-Transition-2020-An-Altman-Weil-Flash-Survey-.pdf
8. *Ibid.*
9. ANALYSIS: *Legal Collaboration Tech Use Is Surging, Surveys Show.* https://news.bloomberglaw.com/bloomberg-law-analysis/analysis-legal-collaboration-tech-use-is-surging-surveys-show

Chapter 2:
Unlocking the power of contractual data

By Shilpa Bhandarkar and Doug Donahue, Linklaters | CreateiQ

Contracts, and the process of creating and negotiating them, represent the most abundant and valuable form of legal and audit data. However, businesses can rarely access or manipulate this data in its current form – linguistic data buried in MS Word and PDF documents. Through the process of standardization and thoughtful digitization, lawyers can start to capture structured and machine-readable contractual data that can then be exploited by AI technologies and form the basis for true automation. These "full-stack" lawyers will be able to provide an entirely different experience and level of service to their clients, partnering with them to unlock valuable business intelligence, spot trends, and proactively prevent issues from arising, all underpinned by accurate and current contractual data.

Defining "contractual" data and appreciating its potential
Contracts are the nervous system of any business. These documents effectively underpin all business relationships – those with shareholders, investors, clients, employees, suppliers, partners and more.

The most critical contractual data is that contained in substantive legal provisions and clauses. It goes without saying that businesses need to know what they have signed up to and what their contractual obligations are at any given point in time. However, even identifying the right clauses is often more difficult than it might appear, an issue exacerbated by market, regulatory, or political events that need this analysis done at scale and to tight deadlines. For example, as part of the interest rate benchmark reform, banks had to identify interest rate clauses across tens of thousands of contracts, and then update the terms to comply with the new regulations. Businesses had to undertake similar analyses in the run up to Brexit.

There is also important intelligence that can be gathered outside of pure legal provisions and in the actual contract negotiation process. Two key areas are audit and compliance, and management intelligence. In an increasingly regulated world, it is critical for global organizations to be able to control and monitor internal approval processes. Aggregated workflow data across contract suites allow chief legal officers to better manage the workload of their teams. It also allows them to gain a better understanding of which provisions are heavily negotiated and in what circumstances, which then allows them to adapt and update their contractual playbooks for greater efficiencies. This time saved to close a contract has a direct impact on business revenue, particularly in the context of sales or trading contracts.

We therefore use the term "contractual data" to describe all of the information contained within a contract, as well as intelligence generated through the contract creation process. It includes information expressed in words (for example, substantive clauses, names of signatories, and descriptions of contract types) or numbers (for example, dates, prices, and thresholds or trigger amounts). It also includes information gathered through the negotiation process – for example, was approval sought to change the substantive provisions for a particular clause and if so, who approved the deviation and when.

Given the volume of data contained in these documents, it should be no surprise that the process of creating, negotiating, and managing contracts can have a significant impact on the financial and competitive position of a business. A recent report by The World Commerce and Contracting Association found that an average of 9.2 percent of annual revenue is lost due to ineffective contract management, such as slow negotiations and missed milestones. This percentage is even higher – at 15 percent – for larger organizations.[1] The corollary is also true – a well-managed, technology-enabled process of managing contracts helps drive revenue, reduces costs, and mitigates against business risk.

Accessibility of contractual data and the need for "structured" data

While written contracts – and the process of contracting – contain an abundance of data, that data is still incredibly difficult to access. This is primarily because the industry is still predominantly using decades-old software to create and store agreements in digital format, but these are basically digital copies of paper documents rather than digital documents. Contractual provisions still have to be extracted from Word or PDF documents and then "translated" into a format that allows for data manipulation and analysis, whether by humans or with the help of technology, and audit trails are invariably lost in multiple email inboxes. This also explains why businesses are largely reactive in looking at contractual data – for example,

M&A deals or planned legal and regulatory changes like Brexit or the phasing out of IBOR rate all need intensive due diligence exercises – rather than proactive in using data to prevent issues from arising or to gain better business intelligence. Becoming more proactive with legal data analysis is a real opportunity for legal teams to become business enablers.

This approach to contracting fails to take advantage of technology that allows for dynamic data access.[2] However, all of this is underpinned by the need for structured contractual data. The most efficient way to capture clean and comprehensive contractual data is to create that data in a structured, machine-readable format from the outset.

Computers largely read quantitative data, represented by numbers, currencies, and binary outcomes. Contracts, by contrast, contain linguistic data – words, sentences, clauses that still require human review before they can be "consumed".

Structured data can be found in clearly defined data types and resides in predefined formats and models, making it easily searchable and machine-readable. Unstructured, linguistic data, on the other hand, is not machine-readable in its natural format and therefore requires human review to extract and retrieve relevant and useful data points.

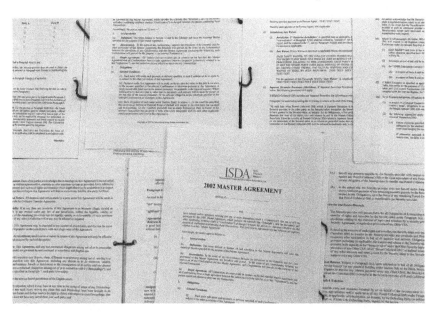

Figure 1: Contractual data today – largely unstructured and therefore requiring human review before it can be translated or manipulated by a computer.

```
    "eligible_securities_substitution_is_applicable":"not_applicable"
},
"substitution_of_principals":{ ⊟
    "is_applicable":"not_applicable"
},
"trade_date":{ ⊟
    "specify_date":"2022-10-22"
},
"additional_termination_event":{ ⊟
    "borrower_termination_election":"not_applicable",
    "illegality":"not_applicable",
    "force_majeure_event":"not_applicable",
    "other_additional_termination_events":"not_applicable"
},
"execution_date":{ ⊟
    "executionDate":"2022-10-21"
```

Figure 2: Contractual data in machine-readable format.

What digital platforms and structured data enable us to do

With each new contract they create, businesses unfortunately continue to add to the repository of unstructured data on a daily basis. More progressive lawyers are choosing to break that cycle, taking a different, more digital, approach to new legal agreements.

Digital contracting platforms such as CreateiQ allow users to create structured contractual data within a single environment, automating key aspects of the process, and capturing business-critical data at each stage. The approach is not to extract data after contracts have been created, but to produce and extract usable data in real-time, as part of the contract

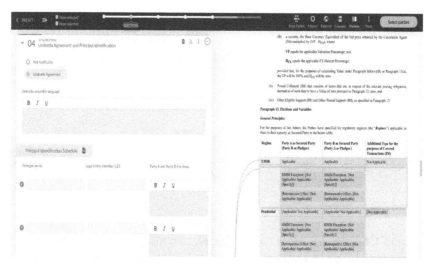

Figure 3: Creating data in a structured format.

creation process. Figure 3 shows what this looks like in practice. On the left-hand side of the screen are pre-defined data fields. As these are selected, it creates the contract, with the traditional documentary view on the right-hand side. Each choice or click has a digital footprint that can be accessed and analyzed, thereby producing a digital audit trail in parallel to creating and negotiating the document.

In addition to creating structured contractual data, there are several other benefits to adopting a digital approach to contracting:

1. *Faster and cheaper negotiations.* Traditional negotiations usually take much longer than they should, with significant amounts of time spent on non-legal tasks like redlining document versions, drafting emails explaining changes, and discussing provisions and approvals across a range of channels. By having a clearly defined process online, negotiations are completed much faster. The reduction in time spent on each contract reduces costs and allows lawyers to spend their time on more high-value tasks.

2. *Reduced legal risk.* Digital platforms allow senior lawyers to create digital playbooks, setting out a clearly defined negotiation process online – for example, requiring approval for deviations from an agreed standard position or including an automatic notification to the Risk team whenever a contract value goes above a certain threshold amount. This allows contract negotiation to be delegated to more junior lawyers with less experience, or even to business colleagues, but without increasing the risk of error.

3. *Greater ability for business teams to self-serve.* Linked to the above, digitized templates, playbooks, and increased transparency mean legal teams can loosen the reins on contract negotiations, allowing commercial, sales, and procurement teams to self-serve many different contract types. This is more empowering for those teams but, more importantly, allows businesses to close contracts faster and bring revenue into their firms quicker.

4. *Mitigating business risk.* In addition to reducing risk at an individual contract level, digital platforms allow legal and businesses to gather and use aggregated contract data to mitigate wider business risk. For example, knowing when significant contracts are due to expire in the next quarter as currencies fluctuate as management are seeing increasing political risk in certain jurisdictions means that teams can inform business decision-making.

5. *Easy collaboration*. Even simple contracts can involve multiple collaborators and layers of sign-off – legal, business, risk, tax and so on. Digital platforms allow all these teams to collaborate and negotiate in one unified workspace, with all edits, approvals, mark-ups, and eventual execution taking place in a single location. This then also provides a "single version of truth" for businesses looking to analyze their contract post-signing, whether for an M&A or other event.

6. *Organizational efficiency*. Digital solutions also allow for better monitored performance with data dashboards that give valuable insights and visibility into workloads and distribution, and where in the contract lifecycle delays are happening.

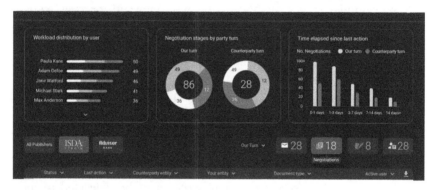

Figure 4: Management dashboards.

What this looks like in practice: Derivatives industry case study – ISDA Create

ISDA Create is a digital contracting solution designed for derivatives documentation and built-in collaboration between the International Swaps and Derivatives Association, Inc. (ISDA) and Linklaters. It digitizes the creation, negotiation, and execution of derivatives documentation for both the buy-side and sell-side, as well as custodians, and is a key part of ISDA's data and digitization strategy, designed to take the derivatives industry to a place where real automation of processes and trades is possible, thereby reducing the risk in capital markets transactions while increasing efficiencies.

The first step is standardization. ISDA put the industry on solid footing by creating and then encouraging the adoption of the ISDA Master Agreement, a common template to negotiate derivatives trading relationships between firms. The widespread adoption of this standardized document removed

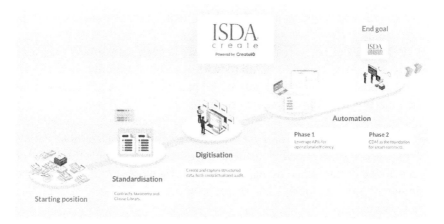

Figure 5: The strategy towards greater automation.

the chaos of having to agree terms when each party has its own preferred form of agreement with its own unique clauses, definitions, and structure. Today, the ISDA Master Agreement is the central legal agreement to every swap trading relationship in the world.

What we have learned over the last few years, during the regulatory repapering exercises the industry has gone through, is that there are currently well over 100,000 swap trading relationships in play, and many new trading relationships are created every year. Progressing from the first step of standardization to the second step of digitizing these agreements and trading relationships is therefore a significant milestone – one that should not be underestimated.

That is where ISDA Create comes in, taking the paper-based standardized documents to the digital world. ISDA Create goes a step further by linking the documentary "human" view that lawyers still desire, to the machine-readable view that the business ultimately needs. In other words, it creates structured data but through a more recognizable process.

In 2021, the ISDA Master Agreement with its accompanying Clause Library was digitized onto ISDA Create. Digitizing the Clause Library involved taking each clause apart to identify all of its component parts (for example, notice periods), categorizing and tagging each of those components (for example, day types), and then identifying the variables for each of the categorized and tagged components (for example, Local Business Days, calendar days). This created a way to identify each clause and every variant of each such clause in the Clause Library by the appropriate tags, like a Dewey Decimal Classification for clauses of the ISDA Master

Agreement, which allows users to quickly identify that two clauses are the same because they have identical tags.

As a result of this digitization exercise, lawyers can now create and, where necessary, customize, the industry's most commonly used clauses to the industry's most commonly used agreement with a few clicks rather than infinite amounts of free-text drafting.

This is significant because it makes negotiations much more efficient – industry participants will have the same inventory of clauses to choose from to accomplish specific business outcomes, plus it avoids the common occurrence of parties bringing their differently worded but substantively similar, if not identical, clauses for a specific business outcome to a negotiation.

More importantly, it maximizes the amount of structured data that can be extracted out of legal documents. Given the volume of these documents that are in circulation at any given point in time, the data sets created are significant – both at an institutional level but also industry-wide.

Creating this pool of structured data has laid the foundation for real automation. Through APIs, users of ISDA Create are already pulling the contractual data they create on the platform into their downstream systems, as well as converting that data into the Common Domain Model that is being developed by ISDA in collaboration with other industry players. In due course, that should lead to a purely digital future with the use and adoption of smart contracts.

What does this mean for law firms?

As legal teams learn to appreciate the value of contractual data and that data becomes more embedded in business processes, lawyers will have to evolve their approach to drafting and negotiating contracts and learn new skills.

Clients will expect legal advice backed by data. Transactional legal advice should become more targeted and will also be provided more quickly as lawyers have more ready access to information. Due diligence processes then become more about information analysis rather than about locating or identifying information. Regulatory advice should also become more effective as lawyers with access to suites of legal documents across many years are able to conduct more macro analysis. This will allow for the more proactive management of risk rather than retrospective remediation. Together, this could change the role in-house teams play in their businesses where technical legal advice is enriched by the combination of legal and commercial data that lawyers now have access to in real time.

To make use of the opportunity this presents, lawyers will have to learn new skills and adapt existing ones. In particular, lawyers will have to learn to draft for digitization – essentially drafting a document in a way that lends that document to digitization and structured data capture. There are parallels to the programming world where, instead of free text drafting, coders use a series of "if then" statements and write long complicated code in modules that can then be neatly fitted together or separated out, as the context requires. Forward-thinking lawyers are already taking inspiration from that approach. Set out in Figure 6 is an extract from the ISDA Digital Asset Definitions that are being drafted in exactly this way.

1.1.1 **NDF Settlement Terms**
    (i)   **IF** the Settlement Price at the Valuation Time on the Valuation Date is greater than the Forward Price,
    (ii)   **THEN** the Seller will pay the Forward Cash Settlement Amount to the Buyer on the Settlement Date,
    (iii) **OR ELSE IF** the Settlement Price at the Valuation Time on the Valuation Date is less than the Forward Price,
    (iv) **THEN** the Buyer will pay the absolute value of the Forward Cash Settlement Amount to the Seller on the Settlement Date.

Figure 6: NDF settlement terms from the draft ISDA Digital Asset Definitions.

This approach also allows the contract to continue as a "living" document rather than one that is executed and filed away somewhere. There is so much potential for "full-stack" lawyers - those who are technically excellent but whose legal skills are enriched by their access to data and their ability to create and analyze it. Once they have access to legal data, they will be able to find efficiencies across the entire contracting process – identifying which clauses or approval processes slow negotiations down; which contracts take an unusually long time to execution; and even which of their advisors provide the best return on investment. Beyond the contracting process itself, risk will be much better managed as they will know exactly what is in their contracts in just a few clicks. Finally, they can make the legal department much better integrated across the business by providing complete contract data exports to any other business system that could benefit from it.

As we move into this new era of the "full-stack" lawyer, where data is at our fingertips and critical to every decision we make, it will not be long before people start wondering how we operated prior to this "golden age" of data accessibility. We fully expect the response to the description of past/current practice to be the same as the response we get when explaining to younger generations about our use of and dependence on the Encyclopedia Britannica.

References
1. The 10 Critical Pitfalls of Modern Contract Management – Webinar Recording & White Paper (worldcc.com).
2. Smarter Contracts and Digital Assets, Reports, LawtechUK.

Chapter 3:
Law firms' approach to talent and the current lack of data collection

By Phil Burdon and Tom Spence, Donoma Advisors

Introduction
"Law firms are late to the business model of using data analytics."
Head of human resources, international law firm

"Data = this is what we are seeing. How can we harness successes or learn from failures if we can't see them?"
Global head of lateral talent, US law firm

A typical law firm spends roughly 70 percent of total expenses on talent, including recruitment, salaries, benefits, training, and retention.[1]

Data and the use of data in the commercial world is clearly not a new concept, but it is increasingly underpinning a greater number and higher proportion of decisions than ever before as companies begin to understand the potential value of such insight. This conversation has become even more relevant following the disruption caused by COVID-19 with remote working significantly altering the way firms engage with their people. With the flexible working dynamic set to remain in some form, we must look to new ways to assess people, and data will play a key role in this.

During this chapter we look to provide insight into the topic of people data within law firms. We appreciate change and innovation within law firms is not an easy journey and touch on some of the challenges that are present whilst also discussing approaches to overcome these challenges.

The legal services industry is often, quite rightly, complimented for being able to react very quickly to client demands and as such often help companies from all sectors face and overcome their challenges. Domestic and global law firms also are able to very effectively help their clients take advantage of growth opportunities. Where law firms are seen to lack the same level of attention and urgency is with regards to internal evaluation and change. This is true also of the speed at which law firms are utilizing data within their businesses compared to other sectors.

People are the foundations of law firms[2] and a key component of growth within the legal sector is through headcount growth, often using recruitment activity or in some cases mergers. To maximize these approaches and their outcomes, firms could use data more effectively to develop a more sustainable, longer term approach to their people strategies and improve the alignment with their growth ambitions.

Across every industry it could be argued that the majority of data-backed decisions are centered on external areas such as assessing the growth of companies' footprint, customer or user acquisition, marketing and advertising spend, amongst others. Naturally, after seeing the benefits of this external focus and as companies have continued to increase the use of data across the board, it has now begun to also underpin decision-making on people within organizations. Whilst law firms are making great strides with regards to utilizing data, it remains a slower adopter than many other industries.[3] This is true also when focusing on how law firms use their people data. It is in this respect that law firms are currently behind the curve.

Law firms have long been using data effectively to assess their client and target client landscape across sectors, practice, and region, which has underpinned client programs, business development strategies, and new market entry. Their client-centric approach to data has led to the use of people data within diversity and inclusion (D&I) strategies largely driven by market pressures and client demands. While there are many critical views of the nature of D&I data and the authenticity of the correlation between the presented data sets and their use, it has been an area where the majority of firms have begun making data-backed people decisions. This, along with the financial performance of partners has been where law firms' relationship with the proactive use of data has, as a widespread theme across the industry, stopped.

What areas of data are currently used in the industry?

If law firms were to create a broader remit for people data within their organizations, there would be a much larger opportunity. Firstly, let's assess where they are currently, with the two aspects where data does play a role in people decisions – financial performance of lawyers and D&I.

Financial performance

Since 2008 and, more recently in the era of widespread implementation of modified locksteps, it would be surprising if there is an area of any law firm's business that has come under more scrutiny than the financial performance of its lawyers, in particular partners.

Financial performance is measured in a consistent way across the industry with origination of client business and the execution of client business being the two main pieces of data that underpin a lawyer's value to a firm. The responsibility for the interpretation of such data most often sits within the management team of the lawyers' practice group, which in turn shares this interpretation with central management, remuneration committees, and partnership acceptance committees.

The consistency with which this data is collected across entire firm partnerships results in a highly valuable tool. This tool allows for data-backed decision-making, which underpins partner compensation, internal promotions, managing modified locksteps, and business development initiatives. As a tool it provides the opportunity to improve the financial performance of an entire firm because the data is consistently gathered and centrally stored.

Why has data within financial performance been successful:

- Top down approach means complete engagement.
- Central importance to the profitability of all firms.
- Accurate and updated dataset.
- Data-driven decision-making.

Diversity and inclusion data

D&I has led to the use of people data being adopted significantly within the legal industry and being a topic of key discussion within firm leadership. One driver has been the demands of clients, which has led to an increased use of data with firms having to provide a confident and data-driven narrative regarding their D&I statistics and strategy.

Why has data within D&I been successful:

- Significant client interest.
- Top down approach means complete engagement.
- Central importance means increased budget and resource.
- Accurate and updated dataset.
- Data-driven decision-making.

A variety of factors have contributed to D&I being one area where law firms have underpinned their strategies with data. Due to the central importance of D&I, in recent years we have seen an increase in resource provided to the area, including the development of industry-specific D&I professionals. Law firms have created specialist roles within their structures that focus on the development of D&I initiatives as well as to be responsible to drive the execution of strategies to meet D&I goals. This has brought greater accountability to the use of D&I data within firms who have invested in such talent.

The use of D&I data to support and shape people and business strategy is just the tip of the iceberg to using people data more broadly. Firms already using this should look at how they can do so in other areas of their people strategies.

Looking at where data is already consistently being used, such as financial performance and D&I, law firms have managed to put people data at the forefront of their strategies. What this shows is that the use of people analytics is very much achievable. There are undoubtedly more opportunities to expand this approach and become more proactive towards the development of data-backed decisions on people.

Is there greater potential to use people data?

"Increasing employee retention is the number one strategy for dealing with today's tight labor market. Add resources to the effort."[4]

"If you don't measure turnover, you can't manage it and you can't learn from it."[5]

In other industries, where people data plays a greater role in organizational thinking and planning, many other processes or areas of the core business are impacted by the use of relevant data. Within law firms there is an argument to say that there is the same potential to expand the use of people data to evolve the way firms approach people processes such as lateral hiring and integration, succession planning, absence and performance management, learning and development, as well as assessing and improving attrition rates for lawyers and non-lawyers.

Areas where data can be used more effectively:

- Lateral hiring.
- Lateral partner integration.
- Third party due diligence.
- Succession planning.
- Attrition rates.

- Absence, holiday, and performance management.
- Learning and development.
- Desirable characteristics, such as collaboration.

People data could also be used to evaluate, test for, and seek certain cultural attributes that underpin stated corporate values. For example, with many firms looking to better collaborate as a major driver for increasing revenues and profits, how many firms are actually assessing their current ability to collaborate, and what role is data playing within this assessment?

While some firms are looking at ways to use data to underpin certain decisions, for the industry at large it appears that more could be done to realize the potential when it comes to using people data to improve their businesses.

Desire for change exists

"Healthy growth is not engineered... It is the reward for successful innovation, cleverness, efficiency, and creativity."[6]

The integration of people analytics should be used to improve efficiencies and outcomes of people processes and aid the overall confidence law firms have in their people-related decisions. What is clear when assessing the legal industry and HR and talent leaders is their appreciation that data should be used to a greater extent, a desire for change, a desire to improve their use of data both from an internal and external perspective.

There are several, consistently discussed, reasons why law firms are often better at reacting rather than looking forwards and with respect to the focus of this chapter, it seems the same hurdles are in-play preventing law firms taking advantage of an opportunity to evolve.

Challenges for change

The role HR plays within law firms

From other research, it appears that in other industries everything to do with data on people specifically sits in HR as a central talent or people function. Big tech is often cited as structuring themselves in this way and in essence elevating the status of HR / talent / people functions. This was perhaps first brought to the fore with "Work Rules – insights from Google".[7] If anything is centralized, it has a greater potential to impact the whole organization, where data on people sits is the same. Law firms are not consistent in this respect. At present, given the use of data on people is fairly nascent within the legal industry, where this area of responsibility and associated budgets sits in the organization is not consistent. Currently it tends to sit either within an often under-resourced HR team or becomes an additional role of a practice group support professional. If data on people as an area is not positioned within a centralized function it will lack the reach and consistency of execution needed to make firm-wide improvements. This will reduce the ability of a firm to determine the whole firm's proficiency to carry out a certain task or to be true to specific values.

COVID-19 has helped the elevation of HR teams in dealing with and managing the fall out of the pandemic, its erosion of firm culture, resourcing issues, flexible working, amongst other significant challenges. Due to this, the interface of HR and leadership has increased and the value of HR teams has had to change as a result. This change in internal perception represents a clear opportunity for HR generally and specifically with regard to the development of data-driven people decisions.

Budget and resourcing
"Resource and budget are crucial and without it data will not follow."
Chief people officer, leading UK law firm

"A lack of data and understanding around people is underpinned by lack of resources and budget to do things properly."
Head of HR, international law firm

As the drive for year-on-year profit increases, law firms are often under-resourced in business services or support teams and as such these areas, in many people's view, do not have the budgets to do more than business as usual activities. This will change as some firms realize the power of data management to improve efficiencies and profitability.

For law firms to capture the potential of the data they have available, a significant challenge to overcome will be that of HR budget and resources for it is these teams that are central to driving change. Despite such a large portion of law firm costs being attributed to their people, there remains a constant theme from within HR and talent teams of being under-resourced and working to tight budgets. It is no coincidence that organizations with larger resource have more appreciation of their people data and how to apply it to the present and future of their firm. Unfortunately, the theme of limited HR budget and resources does seem in part to be attributed to the partnership model within law firms, especially when comparing with industries that are leading the way when it comes to people analytics.

Once an HR team has the resources and budget capable of managing and interpreting the data available, there will be a continual cycle of development as the desire and confidence to create HR and talent decisions based on data output will increase. Whilst change is needed, it is not about starting existing processes and functions from scratch, it is about looking at existing processes through a new lens and to do this HR need to be empowered to do so and law firm leaders will need to be braver with their budgeting to enable this.

Skill sets

In order to fully maximize the opportunity that people data presents for law firms, having the necessary skill sets in house seems logical. However, currently, when law firms see skill set gaps within their HR functions, more often than not, they attempt to "bolt on" these responsibilities to existing team members due to their lack of budget and limited desire to invest. This historical approach is unlikely to enable firms to gain the maximum benefit from the data opportunities available.

The reason being is that, for many within the industry, data literacy is often not a skill set assessed as part of the HR team recruitment process and indeed historically HR departments were not developed with data in mind. As such, law firms often lack the internal skill sets and knowledge to use and interpret the data available and will most likely need to look externally or internally outside of the existing HR function for people with the relevant skill sets to enable and drive the change needed. People within HR need to be educated in how to interpret data output. Data literacy is key – are your people data literate? Do you assess these skills when hiring into HR? Are these skills trained or assessed as part of your teams' employment?

As the concept of people data literacy has yet to reach the industry, there will likely be a new battle for talent in the foreseeable future.

Next battle for talent – data literate business services

Law firms are getting better at recognizing and rewarding the role of non-lawyers within their organizations as firms build more sophisticated business services functions to support their fee earners. In time, the continued rise of "non-fee earner" commercial relevance will likely expand into the need for data-literate people within business services and HR specifically.

As a result, we will likely see a new area of competition for talent emerging within the business and technology services, project management, and data analytics space within law firms. This will not just be centered on those who can use and interpret data effectively but those who can weave data into their firms' longer-term strategic thinking.

Critical factors for success

Implementing change into the way law firms operate is never a quick or easy process. However, change is necessary and the adoption of people analytics is necessary in order for law firms to improve their businesses and how they view and manage their people. Previously we have written that, central to the success of law firms' people strategies, are three key components:[8]

- Leadership;
- Accountability; and
- Consistency.

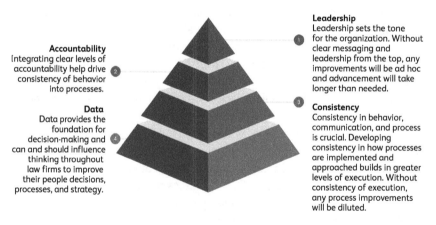

Accountability
Integrating clear levels of accountability help drive consistency of behavior into processes.

Data
Data provides the foundation for decision-making and can and should influence thinking throughout law firms to improve their people decisions, processes, and strategy.

Leadership
Leadership sets the tone for the organization. Without clear messaging and leadership from the top, any improvements will be ad hoc and advancement will take longer than needed.

Consistency
Consistency in behavior, communication, and process is crucial. Developing consistency in how processes are implemented and approached builds in greater levels of execution. Without consistency of execution, any process improvements will be diluted.

Figure 1: Leadership, Accountability, and Consistency.

This model is further enhanced when including data to measure performance and underpin the continual evolution and enhancement of firms' approach to their people and business growth. By using data to provide the foundation, law firms and their leaders can build accountability and consistency across their organizations with more confidence and transparency.

Conclusion

This chapter provides insight into the current and potential role of people data within law firms. What is clear is that there is an opportunity to increase the use of people data within the industry to improve consistency and results in some areas of decision-making. We have tried to identify the main challenges that will be needed to be overcome in order for law firm leaders to make a success of any efforts to do so. By highlighting two areas where people data already underpins decision-making, we have illustrated that it is possible.

We have witnessed a greater desire for data-backed decision-making to touch more areas within law firms. This, along with those in leadership positions looking for more ways to gain buy-in from those who they lead when making important decisions. These two factors mean the scene is set for change.

Making changes to an organization's structure or bringing in new skill sets and assessing new functions is not always straightforward. There is, however, enough evidence through the advances of D&I in particular that means law firms can take advantage of a greater range of people data and associated decision-making.

From the research that helped us frame this chapter and our experience of working with law firms for many years, we would encourage firms to look at this as a central component to their internal structure and in time people data can inform and underpin many aspects of decision-making across firms. To do this it will require central management, right at the top of a law firm's structure to understand the importance and drive the initiative in order for a firm to see the benefits. With the majority of law firm year-on-year spend being on people, it seems that naturally, in time, more will be done to ensure that this spend is well managed and associated decision-making is not purely based on anecdotal data.

References
1 Dr Heidi Gardner and Anusia Gillespie, *Smart Collaboration, Successful strategies to recruit and integrate laterals in law firms*, Globe Law and Business, 2018.
2 A recent report by PwC, assessing global law firms headquartered in the UK, showed that for the top ten firms, 38.6 percent of their costs went on staff (fee earners and non-fee earners), whilst this figure increased to 43.7 percent at the top 11-25. To put this into context, 8.6 percent and 8.1 percent of these firms' costs respectively is spent on properties, representing their second greatest expense. www.pwc.co.uk/industries/law-firms/law-firm-survey-report-2021.pdf
3 www.forbes.com/sites/markcohen1/2019/06/24/why-is-law-so-slow-to-use-data/

4   www.forbes.com/sites/billconerly/2018/01/19/leadership-in-a-tight-labor-market-reduce-employee-turnover/
5   www.delawareinc.com/blog/are-you-measuring-employee-turnover/
6   *Good Strategy / Bad Strategy: The Difference and Why It Matters*; Richard Rumelt.
7   *Work Rules – Insights from Google that will transform how you live and lead*, Lazlo Block, 2015.
8   *Managing Talent for Success*, Second Edition, Globe Law and Business, 2020.

Chapter 4:
Data bites

Joanne Frears, solicitor, Lionshead Law

Definitions and interpretation

I'm a contracts lawyer at heart, so let's start with some definitions.

- *Big Data:* a marketing term that has entered common parlance, meaning unimaginably massive amounts of data from innumerable sources.
- *Data aggregation:* This is not just pooling data, it is the action of compiling data from various sources and preparing it for real world use or summarizing it into an understandable format.
- *Data anonymization:* Scrubbing data so that individuals can't be identified, private information is removed and location and source data is extinguished (unless that is required).
- *Data bias:* an error in data caused by favoring, selecting, or testing or recording one particular outcome over another.
- *Data lakes:* a storage area where data is pooled to create an information swamp. It may help to consider this as a primordial data swamp, from which Smart Data can "evolve".
- *Developers:* people who work with data and know more about it than any lawyer is ever likely to. The following subsets of Developers are included in this definition, but these are subject to change as the field changes and grows. DevOps engineers generally develop platforms to manage data. Data engineers prepare Big Data for analysis and apply it to use cases. Data scientists measure the value of the Big Data models and analysis undertaken by the data engineers. Data strategists find new uses for the Big Data and smart data. Expect to be baffled by these monikers and for them to be used indiscriminately, but also in practice confuse them at your peril.
- *Outlier:* a piece of data that is detached from the main body of

work which may share a source with other data, but which differs significantly from other data and effects a different result or output. Taken from the phrase coined by Malcolm Gladwell in his book Outliers, published in 2008, and not about Big Data.

- *Raw data:* data that has not been structured and is unorganized and generally difficult for humans to read and (crucially) see patterns in.
- *Smart data:* Big Data that is verified, organized, formatted and contextualized so that it is ready to be applied to a Big Data use case.

The singular includes the plural and all pronouns are used interchangeably in the spirit of balance and freedom (after all, *"All data wants to be free"* as Steve Levy sort of once said).

I admit that if I saw the above in a contract, I would despair at the lack of clarity and specificity, but we're talking about Big Data so I hope you'll forgive the broad brush strokes approach!

Finally, under "interpretation", we have also to be aware that not all data is created equally – data science is an emerging discipline, even if it doesn't always seem very scientific or organized.

Big Data

How big is Big Data?
"Big [data], big, huge," as Julia Roberts famously declared.

Google processes nearly 100,000 searches a second (other search engines are available). A second. The are 86,400 seconds in a day or 8,460,000,000 searches (give or take). How do I know that? I searched the internet, because I can, because it's there, and because "it" knows the answer to my question. All of that information is data, of course.

Internet users generate 2.5 quintillion bytes of data every day. It is predicted that, overall, the amount of data generated every day will rise to 181 zettabytes a day by 2025. Being a lawyer, I concede that this type of figure is not my strong suit, but I can tell you that 181 zettabytes is a whopping 10^{21} (or if like me you prefer long-hand, that's 1,000,000,000,000,000,000,000 bytes, or 1 sextillion bytes) or a trillion Gigabytes (i.e. a million millions, or 1,000,000,000,000 or 10^{12}), and it's getting bigger.

In 2021, it would have taken a human around 181.3 million years to download all the information on the internet[1] and that doesn't include time to read it or to gain perspective on its usefulness. Still, to give some perspective, a 2015 study estimated that 15 percent of the video content on the internet is cat-related, and that it would take 2,250,000 lifetimes for a human to download everything on the internet (or 11,312,500 lifetimes for an average cat).

The bigger issue is not that internet data is so heavily feline biased, but that so much of it is unstructured and unchecked data. To be useful it has to be structured and, for lawyers, it also has to be verified and trusted.

Data aggregation

Simply due to scale and also, to some extent, to an anticipation of future use-cases, data is stored and not junked. These massive data repositories of uncatalogued and unstructured data are held for simplicity in vast data storage facilities, known as data lakes. In fact, data lakes and similar data repositories exist in almost all organizations. Think about those bankers' boxes that linger in the corner of a colleagues' office long after they should have been archived; then, imagine tipping all of that paper into a shredder and scale it up again, and you have an idea of raw data in a data lake; now scale it up, again and again and again.

Data aggregation is the process of creating some sort of organization from the raw data or creating a stream off the data lake. Going back to the file analogy, the organized and sub-divided files in marked bankers' boxes, numbered sequentially, were aggregated data, organized into pleadings, witness statements, versions of drafts, due diligence reports, disclosure letters, or any other way of organizing a file so that another fee-earner can pick them up if they need to.

In the legal profession, we have a head-start in terms of conceptualizing Big Data, data aggregation, and data lakes, as we are obliged to organize information received from clients and keep files of work undertaken for our practices. We also have the principle of "precedent" – the original form of Big Data. Precedent requires us to look back at vast tomes of past legal decisions to indicate the likely outcome of further ones and inform arguments in respect of cases. Let's also not forget that, due to the need for social cohesion and societal compliance, we have reduced statutes to writing for centuries. In the legal field then, we "do" Big Data and always have.

Arguably, the difference between precedent and Big Data is simply scale and application and the fact that obviously data lakes of heterogeneous data are now available to all and not simply qualified professionals in specific fields.

In the legal sector, if you want to know a case outcome you can search for it on formal and informal databases, many of which are free, but all of which are structured and cross-relational. Some searches will give you similar cases and some decisions come with interpretation on the facts and the law. This type of data is more structured and, of course, more helpful to the enquirer. This is, to some extent "smart data". Occasionally also in law, we draw on parallel cases in similar fields or on similar facts to guide principles and to prove that a hoped-for outcome is reasonable or desirable. We also draw on examples of outliers in legal decisions that indicate where precedent turned, for better or worse.

For the purposes of this chapter, we are going to focus on the sort of mediated aggregated data sources that come from the legal profession or legal service sources and its wider connected diaspora (such as the insurance industry) and those enterprises that can exchange cohesive data, which means – happily for some – no cat videos.

Big Data, smart data, and value-add

Using Big Data in your firm

The ability to bring together and aggregate data with impacts on and relevance to the legal profession is immense. It brings new opportunities to interrogate data and determine outcomes using it and, as data scientists call this semantics, I think that will chime with most lawyers.

In a recent US case I was involved in, US counsel believed there may be inherent bias in the case being heard in the state where the claimant's business had been established and looked for an opportunity to request that the hearing be moved to another state.

In submitting that advice, the US attorney provided the client with details of the outcome of every case determined by the allocated judge in the state where the proceedings were issued and those of the judges who had the necessary specialism and availability in the listings in the state the client indicated they wished to move proceedings to. The client was presented with comparable cases, outcomes of cases on similar facts, and on ones with similar facts in dissimilar industries, details of where the judges qualified, their professional life prior to joining the judiciary, where their clerks had studied, and who they had worked with.

Based on that information, the client chose to apply for a transfer of the case and was successful. The client then secured a listing with a judge whose background they knew and whose industry-specific knowledge they believed would be more aligned with their respondent's case in this claim and who had recommended judge-led mediation in well over half of the cases they had heard. The client then moved for mediation and the matter was settled.

This is a simple example of the use of comparative data to make an informed decision. It wasn't Big Data, but it was smart and helpful, and provided significant value-add to a case where negotiations had stalled.

Overtly or otherwise, lawyers have been doing this sort of research – reading cases and predicting outcomes then packaging it for clients – for years. Lawyers who are considered great are mostly those that could draw on past knowledge to guide future decisions and who seem to be able to "predict" the outcome of a case simply by reading a file. It is, however, a skill that is learned and not simply an inherent and mythic quality of second sight or indicator of vast intellect.

Now, anyone with access to Big Data can make these evaluations and all law firms should be using data in this way and not relying solely on the partner or associate who seems to have a charmed run in litigation or always seems to be able to predict how a deal will go and swears it's about reading body language.

Are Big Data and smart data a "value add" that lawyers can use to differentiate their practice from other firms? The truth is, it always has been and it should remain so. The key of course is how you choose to use it.

Marketing a firm on the basis that it uses Big Data could be one of your least exciting marketing campaigns ever; right there alongside "we are experts" in its bland self-congratulatory assertions. Marketing your business as "successful in 98 percent of cases" is an attention seeking, interest grabbing winner though, at least initially. People love the certainty of statistics even when they don't fully understand them and if statistics seem inherently trustworthy, a lawyer with good stats is doubly so. That type of assertion and campaign won't last though and the truth will out if the 98 percent comes from only ever managing two cases!

By virtue of their international reach and scale, as well as the number of transactions and client engagements undertaken, large firms have the jump on smaller ones when it comes to transactional history to created proprietary aggregated Big Data. It is not necessary, however, to draw only on your own firm's data to create value-add for clients. The type of hard research into the human elements of law I mentioned above is valuable enough when you can present it to a client alongside additional metrics such as "likely outcomes of court cases in this field" and "average awards" from deal logs and blogs, and insurance providers, as well as across multiple agencies and sectors, versus negative outcomes which may include fines and penalties, accident and injury reports, board reports, and published audits. Add to that precedent, predictive analysis of case outcomes from AI programs readily available and financially accessible to many law firm, and then perhaps even whether a court hearing is environmentally sustainable and what the carbon output of a full trial would be – and the client can then be presented with real choices, determine a risk-based preferred outcome, and make an informed choice about their next move.

The question often is, where do you start? The answer is often not where you think. There are countless sources of Big Data and multiple offerings of AI packages that will provide different types of aggregated data and outcomes and choosing one service to digitize all of the knowledge within your firm to create an X-branded data "pond" or perhaps a larger data lake (depending on the size of your business) will simply involve throwing money at a program and saying, "What next?" until one of the partners says "Enough!". The fact is that there are probably only a few handfuls of lawyers in your region who would even know where to start writing the specification for that work to be commissioned and fewer who would be able to scale the opportunities once it was written.

Enter the developer. You need to get good advice, and the place to get this is from data strategists who can turn your dream of "supreme legal knowledge" into delivered work by engaging with development engineers whose passion it is to teach AI how to interrogate data by using data and whose talents at programming machine learning mean that the programs offered provide not only predictive programs, but outcome thinking.

Expect every sizeable law firm to have data strategists and data scientists as part of their "knowledge" resource by the end of the decade and expect that "tech support" won't just be for the "Help, I think I've broken it" moment when the DMS goes down, but that it will include data engineers who provide case support of the type currently undertaken by armies of paralegals, trainees, newly qualified and associate lawyers. In one act of logging-on, the paper-based research of such teams will seem as arcane as affixing a wax seal on engrossment paper or sewing briefs for counsel.

Data, trust, and confidence in the profession

The death of the trusted advisor
In his excellent book 2019 book, *Online Courts and the Future of Justice*, Richard Susskind[2] cautions that it is not enough to simply replicate the current judicial system by implementing technology to, in effect, mechanize the current, largely broken, system. He warns that the use of technology must be applied in place of the courts, and even the professionals who

advise and profess in them. I agree with the former point but diverge on his latter.

Susskind argues that lawyers are not an inherent or even necessary part of the legal process, and that the role of a "trusted advisor" is not one that needs to be performed by a human. Instead, he anticipates this can be performed by a machine. Yes, it is undoubtedly true that fed with Big Data, AI is excellent at predicting likely outcomes when applied to legal cases in courts. Such programs can divine strategies and could provide accessible, reliable, consistent, and certain outcomes for applicants, but just as there is mistrust of "fat cat lawyers", there is also suspicion and mistrust of decisions made by algorithms.

Even with planned and in force UK, EU, and US accountability for algorithms acts, we still have a long way to go to enforce standards for transparency in such algorithmic decision-making and, more fundamentally, ensuring that Big Data is unbiased when it is used.

Data bias

It is generally recognized that humans have innate bias and so the data that humans record and store will inevitably reflect that bias. That can be as simple as a data search term that becomes embedded in a program or a tick box that is binary in its nature (yes/no, male/female, full-time/part-time). This by its nature creates a problem of ethics in data and therefore credibility for lawyers in the data that they choose to use; how can the outcome ever be "right" if the input was not unbiased and correct? This then begs the question, is Big Data inherently valuable if it is not completely correct?

Unfortunately, like history, data is often supplied and stored by the "victor" – the party in control of the equipment to record and store it, the party who believes it may have a future use, or the one who set the parameters of collection in the first place. Data bias is subtle and it is manifest in a million ways and when that is scaled in Big Data, it becomes pernicious. Without vigilance, the bias becomes embedded as a "norm" and goes unnoticed, until the decision output that is based upon it is delivered and is clearly wrong.

The wider issues of data bias are dealt with elsewhere in this book, by practitioners far more learned on the subject than me, and all contributors to this work have strong views on this subject.

There are very valid concerns being raised, as much by the technology community as by leaden feet Luddites, that if we hand over automated decision-making to AI justice and judges we still may not achieve fairness and consistency because of data bias. Until we can ensure outcomes that are at least as considered, explained, and consistent as those in current human-led courts, "fixing" our justice system by using Big Data and judgment via AI won't be as "smart" as we intend.

The double-bind of confidentiality

It is necessary to recognize that data bias exists throughout raw data sources and also in aggregated data, although one would hope that it has been identified and "cleaned" before use.

Clients also need the reassurance that not only has data bias been identified and made negligible, but also that any law firm data that is used and poured into a data lake has recognizable features of its business, identity, and matter removed and made generic. It is legal practice 101 that client information remains confidential at all times. Clients have to trust that information they provide to their legal advisor is and will always remain confidential and be secure. This is double-bind then; data must be trustworthy and transparent, but legal client data must also be confidential. Smart data is the confluence of the data lake output and aggregated data can address this, but it takes an acknowledgement of both of the fundamentals of eliminating bias and respecting confidentiality to be truly as trusted as it needs to be.

Worldwide spending on Big Data analytics solutions is said to be worth over \$274.3bn (in 2022 figures)[3] and the legal profession as a proportion of this lags far behind other service industries such as insurance. What is clear is that if the legal profession is to use Big Data effectively, the issues of bias, confidentiality, and trust need to be solved.

Learning lessons from other professions

The insurance industry has, perhaps predictably, been an early adopter of Big Data, along with the medical profession. This should not be surprising given that assessing likely outcomes and risk are key in both professions.

In insurance, Big Data and AI are used to analyze and predict trends rather than relying on outdated demographic and social data. It has allowed the industry to use powerful tools that predict customer behaviors, likelihood of claims and buying engagement, as well as to develop new, more targeted, products.

Medtech is massive and segmented, running the gamut of technologies to manage hospitals to those that provide predictive diagnosis, research insights, and lines of enquiry for targeted drug treatment. Wearable medtech already facilitates real-time health tracking and drug administration, all enabled by predictive analysis of Big Data sets.

If we consider the application of Big Data to law, it is easy to see an application for it in "pre-crime", which identifies signaling behaviors and indicates steps that can be taken to prevent a single or multiple signaling individuals from committing a criminal offence or even a breach of contract. Future law practitioners also see applications to the legal system and automated algorithmic justice, not just existing processes "pimped" by AI. Law though, like medicine and insurance, has to deal with life's "what-ifs?" and with those who challenge the status quo and any AI "pre-crime" model would have to factor that in also. We may feel that a sense of justice cannot be programmed in to a machine, but we arrive at that from our own inputs and experiences, just as AI will.

When data bites back

Can a lawyer who has handed over advice to AI avoid responsibility for the output of that program, or shift responsibility onto the technology provider, who provides the means for the advice to be given? Is providing those means sufficient to make the tech company responsible for the output from their program, particularly if the advice seems "bad"?

This naturally raises the question, what is "bad advice"? Whilst some advice might seem to all reasonable people to be "bad", the subjective nature of advice can often mean that it is hard to tell if, in the circumstances, the advice would have been materially different if it had been given by someone else, or whether the application and timing of the advice and the circumstances in which it was given, now make it appear, with even a slight degree of hindsight, to be bad.

What is clear is that if clients are to accept advice based on Big Data or judicial decisions based on algorithmic assessment, they are going to want to ensure that they can seek recompense when the data bites back.

This circles us back to how the insurance industry uses AI and whether it can predict and scope the failings of AI, accept its limitations, and apportion blame to a non-corporeal "thinking" entity such as AI or its supplier. If so, the insurance industry should be able to provide indemnity cover that will allow use of the practical applications of Big Data that the justice system and lawyers need. Whilst this may then seem like a case of "marking its own homework", the insurance industry will need to provide extended or possibly much more specific cover for AI advice or algorithmic decisions when it is not possible to identify the original data source, or even if it is, when the advice output appears to be well-made, but bad advice.

Outliers

At the end, and on the edge of this chapter (as it should be), are "outliers". These are the oddities and peculiar outputs from AI programs. In statistical analysis, outliers are the upper and lower boundaries of information that sit beyond the usual distribution range of expected results. Often, they arise due to human error, experimental errors or skew in the data, or from lack of clarity in the data sets used. Outliers may be discarded when analysis of them is undertaken but there are instances, particularly in AI, where the outlier is outside of the normal expected results but it remains a valid measurement.

Two notable examples of outliers arise in tactical games played against computers. In the 1997 "Re-Match" of Deep Blue v. Kasparov, Deep Blue played an unexpected move that led to Kasparov resigning the match. Kasparov alleged that the move could not possibly have been suggested by Deep Blue and was in fact a play proposed by a rival Grandmaster working with IBM who had overridden Deep Blue to make the play. Further analysis indicated that the move made by Deep Blue was in fact based on a bug; faced with multiple options for play and no clear choice that would lead to a win, the program chose a random move. If the game had continued, it would have resulted in a perpetual check (adding credibility to the "no clear preference" explanation). It was the AI equivalent of rolling a polyhedron decision-making dice!

In 2017, Google's AlphaGo beat world number one Go player, Ke Jie in all three match games. Ke Jie later commented that he was shocked by a move Alpha-Go made that "would never happen in a human-to-human Go match". That move was another outlier – or was it learnt, if unexpected, "behavior"?

Simply because a result is beyond the normal expectation of a human decision does not mean that it is an unreasonable one to make or that it is not a well-considered, evidence-based one either. In these situations, how to deal with an outlier may come down to human intervention and instinct; the spark of the person who can ask "what if it's right?" of insight or possibly even instinct that makes a synaptic connection in a human that is decisive in a strategy.

Sometimes an outlier is acceptably disruptive and informs a new way of working or changes our perspective on how something should be done and, on closer inspection, its validity is clear. Obviously, the decision about how to deal with outliers depends on the use-case, the context of the output, and it requires knowledge of how it was arrived at. Assessing that and the value of an outlier in that context is simply part of the processing process that a lawyer using AI will need to undertake.

When the outlier, or the "Minority Report", is issued, lawyers will need to step forward and be ready, willing, and able to debate it in the real-world based on really good smart data. In this respect, perhaps the future of the legal profession does lie beyond being a trusted advisor and will move to become one of moderator of advice provided by computer.

Now retired from play, Ke Jie commented on AlphaGo's playing capabilities, acknowledging that he had once been its equal but no longer was. He said, "[AlphaGo] sees the whole universe, while what we see is just a pond in front of us". Frankly, I couldn't sum up Big Data and its applications better.

References
1. Unicorn Insights and Tech Jury, https://techjury.net/blog/big-data-statistics/#gref
2. *Online Courts and the Future of Justice*, Richard Susskind, 2019. Oxford University Press.
3. Source: Business Wire.

Chapter 5:
Data in a remote environment

By Silvia C. Bauer, Luther Rechtsanwaltsgesellschaft mbH

Introduction

The world of work has changed with the onset of the COVID-19 pandemic. Employees are increasingly demanding flexibility from their employers – both with regard to working hours and work locations. Many employers have recognized the positive effects of mobile working. These include, for example, higher motivation of employees, increased quality of work due to optimal working conditions, a better work–life balance (especially in the case of severe disability or health-related impairment), increased flexibility that such working time models enable as an important part of the modern working world, and the promotion of environmental aspects by minimizing distances travelled to work. Employers are therefore well advised to increase their attractiveness on the labor market by offering appropriate options.

However, employers have to ensure that their employees remain fit for work – even when they are no longer present in person at the workplace. Although mobile working was quite common before the COVID-19 pandemic, the sudden and in many cases complete withdrawal from the office has caused major challenges for many employers.

Under the term "new work", various models of working together outside the office have already been developed, such as working entirely from home (homeworking), working temporarily from home, teleworking, or simply mobile working. Depending on which model is chosen, this can have different consequences under labor law.

In the – now rather rare – classic homeworking model, the homeworker is given tasks to work on at home. However, he or she is not integrated into the employer's operational organization. This means that the employer has no right of direction with regard to working hours and the execution of activities and must, for example in Germany, observe further regulatory requirements on occupational health and safety for home-based workplaces. More common now are models such as temporary work from the home office or on the road, where the employer provides its IT work equipment, is technically and organizationally authorized to give instructions to the employee, and bears responsibility for the employee's activities.[1]

Whether and to what extent work outside the office is permitted must be regulated by the employer and the employee in the employment contract. If no regulation has been made, the employer can instruct the place of work thanks to its right of direction, or in this case the work must be done in the office. If the home office is contractually permitted, regular regulations must also be made regarding equipment, occupational health and safety, the supervision of the employee and the distribution of costs.[2]

What all models have in common is that data is exchanged digitally. Work orders can be placed and completed at any time and from any place thanks to virtual access to internal company networks, documents are digitally stored, edited, signed, and exchanged, employees coordinate their work via digital conference systems, and processes such as time recording, training of employees, project planning, invoicing, and even the processing of customer enquiries are automated.

A topic that has also often been forgotten and is still inadequately regulated in many cases today is data protection; with work from outside one's own office, the employer has only limited control over its IT work equipment and the data processed with its help. Outside of the office, private and business matters become intermingled. Here, the employer must respect the employee's privacy all the more and thus certain limits are set with regard to controls, right of direction, and so on.

As an employer – and also as a business partner of third parties whose data it processes – it remains responsible for data protection compliance even when processing outside the office. If the employer does not know the requirements to be taken into account and does not implement them, it pays a high price in the case of data loss, data misuse, or similar scenarios. In addition to the heavy fines that data protection supervisory authorities can impose, the loss of reputation must not be forgotten – data protection mishaps are now of high public interest, and regularly reported in the press. In the following, it is explained which data protection requirements a company should observe so that new work leads to a win–win situation for all parties involved.

General data protection requirements
Every company that processes personal data must comply with the requirements of the applicable data protection law. The General Data Protection Regulation (GDPR) has applied to companies based within the European

Union or their branches since 2018. This can be supplemented – if, for example, data of employees is processed – by national regulations that concretize the GDPR.

Admissibility of the processing of data per se

Article 6, Paragraph 1 of the GDPR requires that any processing of personal data must have a legal basis. This applies regardless of whether the processing takes place inside or outside the employer's premises. The person responsible under data protection law for the permissibility of the processing is always the employer.

The employee is subordinate to the employer in the performance of his/her professional activities and acts on the employer's instructions when processing data. This applies regardless of whether he/she performs his/her activities in the office or outside. Therefore, the same requirements for assessing whether processing is permissible or not apply to activities in a home office.[3]

In principle, the employer can therefore refer to its already made assessments of the substantive legal situation regarding the permissibility of processing personal data and does not have to make any new assessments. Deviations may apply if particularly sensitive data is to be processed outside the office, e.g. health data, assessment data, data requiring confidentiality, or if the processing itself is to be classified as particularly critical. The latter may be the case if call center employees carry out video identification or work in the area of online banking. In this case, the employer should carry out a separate assessment as to whether the residual risk of data misuse in the home office is acceptable or whether these activities would not be better carried out in an environment that the employer can fully control. Therefore, in this case, a documented data protection assessment of the risk situation should be carried out.

Other conditions for the processing of data

The implementation of data protection compliance in a company requires that – in addition to the requirements regarding, for example, the documentation of processing activities, the performance of data protection impact assessments, or the introduction of processes for dealing with data protection incidents – the principles standardized in Article 5 of the GDPR are implemented. The company must provide evidence of the implementation.

In addition to the examination of the lawfulness of processing already described above, the GDPR also requires compliance with the principles of purpose limitation, data minimization, storage limitation, and the principle of transparency. As the controller, the employer must also ensure adequate data security. The last point in particular is significant in the context of remote work and requires closer consideration.

General requirements for technical-organizational measures

To ensure the security of the processing of data, each company must implement appropriate technical and organizational measures in accordance with Article 32 of the GDPR to ensure the protection of personal data against unauthorized access, unlawful processing or disclosure, and accidental loss, alteration, or destruction. This includes, in particular, the implementation of measures to ensure a level of protection appropriate to the risk of the processing in terms of confidentiality, integrity, availability, as well as resilience of the IT systems and databases and so on. Ensuring confidentiality is usually implemented through access control and separation control measures. The requirements for integrity are implemented through measures for transfer control, input control, and order control. Measures to implement availability and resilience are, for example, measures concerning the regular archiving or back-up of data, the securing of access and also a control of the measures. Usually, these implemented measures are described in separate concepts. Their compliance must be regularly checked by the employer.[4]

In addition, when introducing or operating IT systems, companies must also take into account the principle of data privacy by design and default, under Article 25 of the GDPR. This is intended to ensure, among other things, that only necessary data is processed and deleted in a timely manner and that this is ideally done automatically.

Obligation to provide evidence and guidelines

According to Article 5, paragraph 2 of the GDPR, every company must be able to prove compliance with the above-mentioned data protection principles at any time. This requires comprehensive documentation on the one hand of the measures taken, but on the other hand also comprehensive documentation on how the company encourages the employee to implement and comply with them. The latter is usually ensured through guidelines or rules of conduct that the employee must comply with.

With such regulations, a company can free itself from legal liability risks if the employee violates data protection regulations in their home office or while working on the move. In addition, employees are made aware of data protection issues through a corresponding regulation. The regulations can be designed either as an addendum to the employment contract or – in Germany, for example – as a works agreement.[5] In any case, they should be binding and formulated in a way that is easy for the employee to understand.

Regulations for technical-organizational measures for mobile working

Regulations on working in a home office or mobile working should, among other things, specify the requirements for the workplace itself and give employees clear instructions on how to deal with company property and the data processed using it. The aim should be to clearly inform employees about which end devices they are allowed to use, when, and under what conditions.

The regulations should also include clear guidelines on how to deal with private technical devices, such as mobile phones, in the workplace and potentially prohibit their use. Private devices usually also store private data that could come into contact with business data. This increases the likelihood that private and business data could be mixed. This should be avoided, as in this case the employer loses sovereignty over its own data due to restrictions on access to the data stored on the private device. The employer may also delete the employee's private data without authorization and could find itself exposed to a claim for damages. It is also critical that the employee could delete business data by mistake.[6] In addition, the maintenance, installation of updates and so on of the private device is regularly the responsibility of the employee; here the employer can no longer ensure that the necessary and appropriate technical-organizational protective measures are installed on the device. As a rule, private measures will not meet the same standard as company measures.

In addition, a corresponding policy should regulate how employees are to proceed in the event of data protection incidents, IT security incidents, the loss of work equipment, or similar incidents.

Even if it is primarily a matter of digital activities, analogue aspects must not be left out – security incidents initially concern system malfunctions or the disclosure of information by unauthorized third parties, unauthorized access to the hardware or software provided, or the infestation of the hardware or software provided with viruses and other malware, but also the loss of work equipment or data carriers or documents provided. If the employee throws printouts into the paper waste, this can also lead to a not insignificant data protection incident.[7]

In the following, individual requirements that should be the subject of such a guideline or regulations on conduct are listed by way of example.

Requirements for the workplace

Even in the remote office, the employer must ensure that third parties cannot access the work equipment provided or, for example, read or listen in on unauthorized data. Otherwise, confidentiality and data protection will not be maintained.

The following points, for example, can be considered as measures to be specified in a corresponding guideline or as a code of conduct:

- The home office must be set up in a closed room to which no third parties have access during working hours.
- All windows and doors of the room must be closed (potentially locked) when leaving the workplace; if necessary, the home should also be secured.
- The eavesdropping of telephone calls by third parties must be counteracted by appropriate measures, e.g. by closing all doors and windows of the room in which the home office is set up.
- It must be ensured that smart home systems (e.g. Alexa, Google Home, etc.) cannot "listen in" on operational information.
- The screen of the workstation must be positioned in such a way that it cannot be seen by third parties, e.g. through windows.
- Business correspondence (emails, documents, etc.) that is accessed on a laptop or smartphone, for example, must not be read or processed in public in such a way that third parties could become aware of its content.
- Laptops shall be provided with a privacy screen for the display.
- Work equipment must be supervised or carried in areas accessible to the public.
- When not in use, work equipment must be locked or the automatic lock screen must be set up.
- Work equipment or documents must be kept in a safe place (e.g. a lockable cupboard or room) during longer absences and after the end of working hours.
- If the laptop is stored off the business premises it should be in secure storage, e.g. in a hotel safe.
- Passwords must be kept secret.
- No documents may be accessible to third parties.
- No copies may be made in the home office.

- Paper documents that are no longer needed (e.g. old drafts or notes) must not be disposed of in household waste but must be transported back to the office and properly destroyed there (exception: the documents can be made unrecognizable at home by a shredder with high security standards).

Requirements for the technical implementation of the activities in the home office

In order for the employer to retain control over its data and ensure that it is processed in compliance with data protection law, the following regulations are recommended as a minimum:

- The use of third-party or private equipment is prohibited. Only work equipment provided by the employer and whose use or standards it can control may be used. Otherwise, the employer cannot ensure the unauthorized outflow of data.
- The downloading of private software on work equipment is prohibited.
- Software may only be installed by the IT department. Necessary updates must be carried out regularly.
- Maintenance and repair of work equipment provided by the employer shall be carried out by the employer and at the employer's expense.
- Technical modifications to the work equipment provided are prohibited.
- No deactivation or circumvention of technical security measures.
- If the device is lost, the data can be deleted remotely by the employer.
- The storage/processing of business data shall be carried out exclusively using the work equipment provided.
- Business information is stored on the employer's designated infrastructure. This is automatically backed up on a regular basis as part of the data backup concept. If access is not possible, the information can be backed up locally and must be transferred to the employer's designated infrastructure in a timely manner. Local backups must be deleted immediately after they have been successfully transferred.
- No forwarding of business correspondence to private mail accounts, etc. Business communication takes place via secure connections, i.e. corporate access.

- Exclusive use of encrypted USB sticks and no storage of confidential data on a USB stick.
- All work equipment must be secured against unauthorized access with at least password encryption. Neither passwords nor means of communication may be made accessible or handed over to third parties. Passwords or other means of access to the work equipment must be stored securely.
- The private use of hardware and software provided to employees for official purposes is expressly prohibited.
- The employee is obliged to inform the employer immediately after becoming aware of any malfunctions or damage to the work equipment or software made available to him as well as in the event of loss or theft of the work equipment made available to him. The employee shall be liable for the damage, loss, or theft to the extent provided by law.
- Upon termination of mobile working, as well as upon termination of the employment relationship, the employee shall return the work equipment provided to him/her to the employer at the latest on the last day of mobile working or on the last day of the employment relationship. A right of retention should be excluded.
- Attachments in emails from unknown senders should be checked separately and only opened if the sender's name and email address appear confidential.

Data exchange

The company must ensure that it has control over the ways in which data is exchanged between employee, employer, or third parties. Usually, the transport of electronic documents takes place through remote access from the home mobile office, which is appropriately technically protected. Here, connections via a VPN, suitable password protection, two-factor authentication if necessary, the use of management device systems and the use of encryption techniques are usually considered.[8]

If, for example, cloud solutions from third-party providers are used, it must be ensured that the necessary contracts under data protection law have been concluded with them. The controller should have examined the providers and selected them with regard to compliance with data protection law and the implementation of appropriate technical and organizational measures. This initially includes the conclusion of data processing agreements in accordance with Article 28 of the GDPR. If the third-party provider is based in a so-called unsafe third country, i.e. a country that does not have an adequate level of data protection according to the requirements of the European Union, additional guarantees according to Article 44 of GDPR that legitimize this transfer must be given. These can be, for example, the standard data protection clauses together with the implementation of transfer impact assessments including the securing of additional technical and organizational measures that protect the data from unauthorized access. If sensitive data is processed, it should be carefully examined whether storage within the European Union could be considered as an alternative. This applies in particular because the European data protection supervisory authorities and also the courts are currently rather critical of transfers to insecure third countries.

Control rights for mobile working
Employers regularly want to ensure that employees are as productive on the move as they are in the office. This leads to a need to monitor their activity in order to check this productivity or the activities of their employees. Such monitoring is sometimes technically possible by checking log files, real-time usage of IT systems, or similar data. In this case, the employer should carefully check whether this monitoring is actually permissible under data protection law or whether it goes further than the law allows. The monitoring of working time per se will regularly be permitted, as compliance with working time regulations is an obligation under the employment contract; however, a measurement of productivity or work activity – i.e. a comprehensive monitoring of the employee's performance or behavior – will meet with data protection concerns if it exceeds the limits of reasonableness. In Germany, it would only be permissible without a reason if there were concrete, verifiable suspicions of a possible breach of duty (e.g. working time fraud or similar).[9]

A need for control can also arise from the fact that the employer, as the person responsible for data protection, wants to check whether the employee in the home office is complying with company regulations on mobile working that he or she has set. It is always critical here that, at least in Germany, Article 13 of the German Basic Law guarantees the inviolability of the employee's home. Nevertheless, it is advisable for an employer to reserve a right of access to the home office workplace. Only in this way can he adequately check compliance with data protection and occupational health and safety regulations, for which he himself is responsible. In Germany, a direct statutory right of access only exists for certain representatives of the authorities and not for the employer; this is derived from the general requirement of consideration and is regularly contractually agreed.[10]

Conclusion

Remote work can be implemented in terms of data protection law and has become an integral part of everyday business life. However, in order to avoid increased liability risks for any of the parties involved, contractual and organizational regulations should be created that clearly stipulate for both sides what and who is allowed to do with what data in the context of mobile work and how they are to protect it.

The employer must develop and implement concepts for technical and organizational measures that specifically take into account the particular risks of mobile working and the associated loss of control for the employer. In addition to the rules of the game for the employee, this also includes technical measures to be implemented by the employer that enable the secure storage of data as well as their secure transport and exchange. This also includes the prohibition of the use of private work equipment and the contractual agreement of possible controls of the employee during mobile work in the home office.

A binding framework for the proper handling of personal data and the data protection-compliant use of work equipment outside the office should be created with corresponding guidelines. The goal must be to implement effective data protection management for minimizing threats or harmful events. This will ensure the proper processing of data by the company, minimize the risk of data protection incidents and the associated loss of trust among customers or other affected parties.

References

1. Individual Labour Law, Hoppe Kramer, IT Labour Law, 2nd edition 2019, margin no. 616, and Picker, NZA supplement 2021, 4.
2. Individual Labour Law, Hoppe Kramer, IT Labour Law, 2nd edition 2019, margin no. 621, margin no. 628.
3. Paal/Pauly, DS-GVO, BDSG, 3rd edition 2021, Introduction, margin no. 25.
4. Suwelak, ZD 2020, 561, 562.
5. Dury/Leibold ZD-Aktuell 2020, 04405.
6. Verheyen/Elgert, K&R 2020, 476.
7. Suwelack, ARP 2021, 230, 231.
8. Paal/Pauly, DS-GVO BDSG, 3rd ed. 2021, before Art. 1 DS-GVO margin no. 28; Suwelak, ARP 2021, 230, 232.

9 Suwelack, ARP 2021, 230, 233.
10 Individual Labour Law, Hoppe Kramer, IT Labour Law, 2nd edition 2019, margin no. 651, 652.

Chapter 6:
Using data to drive your marketing and business development efforts

By Yolanda Cartusciello, PP&C Consulting

We believe we know our clients and potential clients. Lawyers tell law firm marketers that they know what interests and drives those clients. Marketers know what's important to them on this project because they read the RFP, perhaps sat in on an introductory call prior to the pitch, and did a ton of research on the potential client and assignment. We developed our proposal to speak directly to those factors. *Yet, we lose those opportunities to other firms a large percentage of the time.*

So, we ask them – what did we get wrong? What did we misunderstand? How could we have approached this differently? And, sometimes they tell us (to the best of their ability), and of course they usually sugar coat things a bit. And, we use this information to change our approach, to modify our process, to refine our proposals. And, we'll get better. Next year we'll win more. *But, still, we lose more than we believe we should.*

Has this feedback loop ever played out in your law firm? I know it has through the years in many firms. Of course, the particulars may be different from law firm to law firm. But the loop is the same.

And, here's what's wrong with it – we're listening, but only with our ears. We should be listening to the data around everything we do to attract a new client and land a new project. There's plenty of data available. We just have to look for it and listen to it.

Learnings from data: people say one thing and do another
Data can tell us what people actually do; not just what they say they do.

Decades ago, retailers and manufacturers learned a hard lesson – people say one thing and do another. In the book *Why We Buy, The Science of Shopping*,[1] author Paco Underhill explains that, when faced with a purchase decision (large or small), people behave erratically. When asked why they behaved as they did, their answers rarely matched their actions. Retailers began to hire ethnographers and social behavioral scientists to observe and record behavior. What do people actually do in a retail environment?

What do they do leading up to a purchase? How do they behave differently when they choose not to buy? Many of those marketers' expectations of what people would do proved to be terribly wrong. (This work by retailers was the pre-cursor to Customer Journey Mapping.)[2]

On the web, ethnography has morphed into analytics. But the premise is the same. Rather than ask people why they did what they did, we observe and learn through the data available to us online. Online retailers jumped on this quickly for obvious reasons – they actually sell things on their websites so analytics lets them study the specific activities that lead up to a purchased (or abandoned) shopping cart. As a result, today's retail marketers are highly data-driven.

Yet, most law firms still act as if they are largely indifferent to data. After all, it's a relational business, people within firms argue, and the exact moment a client commits, and the exact motivation behind it is almost impossible to identify. What can data possibly teach us? Isn't "data-driven marketing" just the next catchphrase in legal marketing? Yet, much of what happens around the moment of client commitment can increasingly be observed through data. In fact, there's useful data all around us. Data we can use to:

- Inform our content marketing efforts.
- Plan our business development activities.
- Improve our "go/no go" process.
- Shape our proposals and interviews.
- Improve service delivery.

The balance of this chapter will take a brief look at each of these five areas.

Bringing data into content marketing

Analytics data can help you measure and improve all aspects of your content effort.

Like it or not, when we speak of business development, we must acknowledge that hiring decisions are influenced by the reputation and brand of the firm and lawyers. In the same way that you can't get mad at a scale for reading out your weight when you step on it if you haven't put in the exercise to affect those results, you can't get upset when people have a different view of the firm if you haven't put in the hard work to change that perception. One of the best ways to change that perception is thought leadership. The magic of thought leadership is the essence of showing, not telling. (Example: Law Firm A has put out 20 readable and relevant pieces in the last six months on this subject. I now have a more favorable view of Law Firm A.)

If your firm is a veteran thought leadership marketer, then there's a good chance you've already got the makings to make data a critical part of your effort. Yet, for many firms (and not just the ones making the transition to a marketing approach based largely on knowledge sharing), analytics have probably not become a large part of your team's effort.

For content marketing, Google Analytics and Google Webmaster Tools are wonderful sources of data. There are also myriad other products on the market to help you manage your content and understand your analytics. There are also terrific outside consultants who can help you in this endeavor. No matter what technology or service you use, these are the questions you should be looking to answer:

- Are we increasing the visibility of the firm? More specifically, are more people visiting and interacting with our site than in previous periods?
- Are prospects and clients finding us? Or does the majority of our traffic appear to be potential hires? (You can gauge this pretty quickly simply by looking at your site's top landing pages.)
- Is our content getting found online? Is our search traffic increasing?
- What content types and topics are performing best? Why?
- What types of content and search strings are we most likely to get found for? Are we getting found for the topics where our knowledge and experience is most valuable? If not, why not?
- Where do clients most likely arrive on our website? (Hint: it's less and less frequently the homepage, especially now that online users can more easily access the ever-visited bios more directly). Have we established a clear direction for them to proceed into our website so they can understand our firm, its knowledge, its perspective, and its experience?

To be clear, analytics *should not drive* your content strategy. It should *inform it*. The most successful thought leadership marketers focus first on developing their ideas and building great content and recognize SEO as a downstream activity. But, once again, how people behave online should inform the decisions we make about where and how to invest our content marketing resources. Put differently, a wonderful, unread 20 page article is a waste of time and talent; no amount of data analytics and brilliant content marketing will change the cultural attitudes of an audience with the attention span of a hummingbird. Therefore, such analytics can not only help you shape your content strategy, it can help you demonstrate to those creating the content that their approach may need to be altered.

Using data to inform business development

Behavioral data can help you make your proactive business development efforts more efficient and effective.

The role of business development in a law firm is to establish new working relationships with a number of clients on a number of quality projects in a given year. In some law firms, it might be as few as just two or three. In others, given the practice mix and financials, the number may need to be much higher. Every single new prospective client will interact with your website in some way prior to hiring you. Guaranteed. Most will interact with your website before even speaking to you. Yet, a mid-sized law firm can generate tens or even hundreds of thousands of website visitors in a year. Your job is essentially to find that handful of new clients through a sea of website visitors.

Some will simply jump up and raise their hand. Others will require proactive outreach and hard work. For this latter group, where do you start? Traditionally, business development started with a Rolodex. Who do they know? But, a seasoned partner may have hundreds or thousands of business relationships. How do they prioritize? Alphabetically? (Don't laugh at that last sentence. I know many a firm that insisted on starting call lists by reviewing Rolodex contents alphabetically.) Maybe the place to start is where the data you're collecting directs us.

First you will need a marketing automation system to capture that data. Marketing automation systems can provide *behavioral data* on individual targets. They can provide a range of useful insight such as when they interacted with your site, how frequently they came back, and what interests them (based on their actual behavior). At its core, a marketing automation program should offer you the following functionality:

- Email marketing and metrics.
- User tracking and micro analytics (of both known website visitors and anonymous ones).
- Lead scoring – the ability to score website visitors based on both demographics (who someone is) and behaviors (activities and actions performed by a user on your website or in your social channels).
- Lead nurturing – the ability to execute automated email programs in response to a user's behavior on your site (or their lead score) and nurture them through the buying process.
- CRM integration – any automation program should provide integration into your CRM so useful information captured within your marketing programs becomes readily available and useful to your business development team.
- Forms and landing pages – the ability to create custom forms and landing pages easily and "on-the-fly".
- Progressive profiling – with marketing automation, no website visitor should have to share the same information twice. Progressive profiling lets you collect small bits of information from a user every time they return to your site to access different pieces of content. Done correctly, progressive profiling lets you get just the right information you need to identify your ideal targets.
- Performance measurement – automation makes measuring the meaningful outcomes (leads, opportunities and revenue) of your marketing campaigns both realistic and achievable.

The world of data useful to informing business development strategies is not limited to the information that you are able to capture through engagement with your website or marketing campaigns. Indeed, limiting yourself to what your firm can capture on your own could, arguably, simply feed into a wider, more complex version of the same loop we're trying to avoid. The external data that we can now use, from widely available economic research to bespoke external surveys, is myriad. Combining behavioral data and externally available data and *external research on likely demand and trends* enables a marketing and business development team to work together to:

- Identify a short list of priority prospects based both on a combination of past relationships and demonstrated interest in what the firm has to say and has done.

- Identify a short list of industries, by gauging the level of interest to specific areas of the website (especially industry-specific resource centers) and gauging the traffic from individuals within specific industries. Such work can be supplemented and refined when combined with external data and surveys. Those industry trends, revealed through data analytics, can help you better understand your firm's appeal within a particular sector.
- Tailor interactions and conversations towards what appears to most interest any individual prospective client.

Combining information from generalized sources with the behavioral data we've discussed thus far is not simply a matter of capture and compare. You will need to use a triangulation strategy to layer all available information and make some assumptions about likely behavior going forward. While not a perfect science, it does allow us to get closer to data-driven strategies, and make it less likely that your firm ends up in the "I just want to pitch it this way because my one client thinks it's a good idea" loop of behavior.

Using data to inform the "go/no go process"

Behavioral and historical data can help you make better business decisions.

I've looked at a number of "Go/No Go" tools and strategies used by law firms to determine whether or not to propose on an opportunity. While all are well-intentioned and some are very effective, they're all based entirely on the project leader's perceptions of the prospective client. Some of the metrics are entirely objective (such as location of the project, type of assignment, or alignment with the firm's strategic plan). Others are entirely subjective (strength of relationship, likelihood of getting the work). What's lacking in every tool I've seen is hard data.

Looking ahead, an effective "go/no go" process should include data that comes out of your firm's marketing automation and CRM system. This could include things like:

- *Site engagement* – how frequently has the target interacted with our firm's thought leadership and website presence over the last six to 12 months?
- *Previous win rates* – how does our past success stack up on projects of this type, with this client, in this industry? How does this particular lawyer perform on pitches?

- *Overexposure of sensitive information; intention of the target* – how many times have you proposed special discounts and other financial arrangements in RFP responses recently and how often have you won those proposals? If you're losing an awful lot of them, then consider whether these potential clients are using your firm as a stalking horse, just to gather billable rate information and other financial data to squeeze their preferred firm for a discount. Remember, clients and potential clients collect data too – likely much more than your firm does – and their intentions may not always be aligned with your firm's best interests.

While the actual go/no go decision will always be subjective, the firms that embrace the hard data underlying their past successes and failures will drastically increase their future likelihood of success.

Using data to improve proposals and interviews

Behavioral data can help you craft better proposals.

Once again, a marketing automation system can be a wonderful tool to help a firm develop more effective proposals and interview strategies. Specifically, the system can tell you:

- Which topics and thought leadership a prospect has had the most interactions with over any defined period of time.
- Which projects a prospect has spent the most time with online.
- Which firm leaders and people profiles a prospect spent the most time viewing.
- All this information should be used to organize, plan, and prepare the proposal.

Increasingly, we can go one step further once a proposal is delivered. Some law firms have embraced sales automation tools like Tinderbox, so that the firm can extract data related to how a prospective client actually consumed and interacted with the proposal. Assuming your proposal is delivered electronically (which, more and more are), the system can tell you:

- How much time the various members of the prospect's selection team spent with the proposal.
- Which sections and pages were read the most and by whom.

All this information can be used to shape the priorities and details of a post-proposal interview (if one exists). It can also be used as learnings to improve future proposal development.

Using data to improve service delivery

Data from client feedback programs can help you fix relationships before they run completely off course.

I am a staunch believer in client interview programs and satisfaction studies. I know that there are a good percentage of firms that are still resistant to this concept and therefore I want to tread lightly and not stomp on what will still be a gigantic step for most firms when they first engage in these efforts. However, the problem with most law firm client satisfaction studies is they poll clients at intervals convenient to the firm, often well after they've actually worked with you on a project, and not necessarily at a point in time when the client is most likely to have useful information. Because of this, clients who are well-intentioned are likely to offer only minimal useful information so long after the engagement is complete. Additionally, the questions hardly ever engage the client in a discussion about their own journey from beginning to end. As a result, the surveys measure quality of service through the rearview mirror, but don't actually help the firm improve day-to-day service delivery in a meaningful way.

While firms could engage in a true client journey mapping exercise in which they do ask meaningful and helpful questions about the client's journey directly after an engagement, some firms are engaging in mini-check-in interviews during the engagement. This allows them to ask for specific feedback at various points of the project. The data that comes back from this approach enables firms to:

- Identify points of client frustration long before they become relationship killers;
- Improve performance within specific projects and project phases before it's too late; and

- Aggregate data over time to better understand the firm's performance at all phases within the delivery of a project.

The new data frontier

Lean into data before your competitors lean into you.

Five years ago, I began proselytizing to law firms that they better wake up and embrace client journey mapping before they fall woefully behind more nimble, forward-looking peers. Now, I'm proselytizing again on data. If your law firm is not leaning into the data underlying both your marketing and business development efforts now, in a few years you will find yourselves with declining win rates and a sense of frustration as you try to play catch up with your more assertive and nimble peers.

References
1 *Why We Buy, The Science of Shopping*, Updated and Revised for the Internet, The Global Consumer and Beyond, Paco Underhill, Simon & Schuster, 2009, pp 23-24.
2 For more information on how customer journey mapping may be applied to law firms, see *Business Development in the New Legal Ecosystem*, Chapter 11: Mapping the Client Journey in the New Normal, Yolanda Cartusciello and Bob Robertson; see also *The Client Experience: How to Optimize Client Service and Deliver Value*, Chapter 3, *Cultural shift or cultural shove? The challenges of the client journey in the post-pandemic era*, Yolanda Cartusciello.

Chapter 7:
Analyzing data to increase efficiencies – the client's perspective

By *Mori Kabiri, InfiniGlobe LLC*

Data is one of the most powerful resources in the world, answering critical questions while uncovering hidden insights. In the legal industry, both law firms and their corporate clients collect and analyze data to aid in planning, strategizing, and decision-making.

Firms evaluate data collected from time tracking systems, client feedback, court decisions, contracts, and legal histories to pinpoint, measure, and leverage specific KPIs (Key Performance Indicators) to gauge their revenue, reputation, and growth.

At the same time, clients take advantage of data to control cost, operate more efficiently, and provide better services to their internal customers. Their data is often collected from case information, eBilling data, internal vendor reviews, invoices, budgets, reports, time tracking, etc.

While clients and firms share common goals, such as improving efficiencies, they also differ in other objectives such as reducing cost vs increasing revenue. Although this may seem like a conflict, it actually creates a unique opportunity for firms that take the time to put themselves in clients' shoes to understand client objectives and goals. Using this "inside knowledge", firms can focus on improving performance in meaningful ways, which will be an important factor in vendor evaluations and is integral to building strong and loyal business relationships.

What are metrics, KPIs, and KRIs?
Before we dive into the details, some definitions.

Metrics
Metrics are criteria we can measure; a value or a quantity. Metrics can be a count of records and simple sums, or can be painstakingly filtered or calculated to be as meaningful as possible. Some examples of simple metrics in a corporate legal department are:

- Number of total cases.
- Number of closed cases.
- Number of vendors.
- Number of in-house attorneys.
- Percentage of staff turnover.
- Outside counsel cost.

KPIs

A Key Performance Indicator (KPI) is a quantifiable measure used to evaluate the success of various objectives, which can be a metric or can be calculated using a combination of metrics. All KPIs are metrics, but not all metrics are KPIs. Think of it this way, everything starts with metrics, but when metrics specifically measure the achievement of a desired state, those metrics can be referred to as KPIs. In many client legal departments, the general counsel sets objectives, which guide the legal ops team as they collect and analyze data to generate KPIs that will accurately measure progress and identify opportunities for improvement. Some examples of KPIs in a corporate legal department are:

- Average cost to close case.
- Percentage legal spending from company revenue.
- Percentage legal staff per employee ratio.
- Number of transnational cases per attorney.
- Number of hours spent per case by attorneys.
- Number of days to close non-trial cases.

KRIs

A Key Risk Indicator (KRI) is a metric that provides an early warning for increased risk exposure. For example, a high level of average "% Case budget variance" can indicate problems in estimating effort, scope creep, and so on. If KRIs are not monitored and mitigated in a timely fashion, they will likely result in unexpected fees and expenses and can build discomfort or tension in business relationships. Some examples of KRIs in a corporate legal department are:

- Percentage legal spending from company revenue.

- Percentage legal department budget variance.
- Percentage of cases successfully solved.
- Percentage of budgeted cases handled within budget.

What's the report on reports?
Based on industry and objectives, clients often run a spectrum of different types of reports. Here are some popular reports:

- Case Inventory Management Performance.
- Resource Management Performance.
- Financial Performance.
- Rate Management Performance.
- Invoice Submission/Review Performance.
- UTBMS/Task Performance.

These reports have two primary audiences:

- Senior management – rarely need or want deep, detailed, granular information. They want information summarized at a much higher level, giving them an understanding of department performance at a glance, such as the number of open matters by legal practice group. If these birds-eye-view reports are disproportionate, the CEO and CFO are likely to require an explanation as to the increase in matters and request an action plan from the GC and the legal ops manager.
- Responsible legal managers – need information segmented at more granular levels in order to identify what criteria are driving results and why. Such reports might identify one or more drivers of an increasing case load such as an influx of cases, longer case life, or failure to enter closure information into the matter management database. For them, data drives action.

During process improvements, client legal ops teams will need to answer the following questions:

- What reports and metrics are most important to us and to management? What purpose does each serve?

- How is data being collected, stored, and how easy is it to retrieve?
- What are the criteria for each metric, and can they be defined in a more meaningful way?
- Who is the audience for each metric and what do they care about?
- Can these metrics be repurposed and applied in any other contexts?

Where to source the freshest data
Among the wide array of legal technology, eBilling tools are crucial to generating data-rich sets of legal department business intelligence. Since the 1990s and the birth of legal eBilling, clients have been consistently capturing detailed invoicing information from law firms and vendors, such as the following:

- Matter – name of the matter, project, dispute, or case.
- Type – is this a fee or expense?
- Timekeeper – name of each person billing time.
- Role – the timekeeper's title/level (for example, partner, associate, paralegal, etc.).
- Quantity – time billed per task.
- Rate – hourly rate per task.
- Service date – date the work was performed.
- Description – a textual description of the work performed or expenses incurred.
- Code – UTBMS activity and task codes assigned to each line item.

Clients use information at the invoice level to analyze law firm billing practices, review increases in rates, keep track of what tasks are being performed, and so on. Clients normally select a set of UTBMS codes for their firms to use to improve consistency and quality in coding line items and tracking project status. Clients leveraging AFAs (Alternative Fee Arrangements) also work with their firms to utilize shadow billing to conduct performance verification and generate similarly valuable eBilling data.

The other primary source of data is Matter Management Systems, aka MMSs or ELMs (Enterprise Legal Management) that capture critical matter-related data, such as the following:

- Number / Code – a unique identifier for each matter, project, dispute, or case.
- Category – matter type, can also include practice area.
- Case status – open, closed, pending, etc.
- Firm(s) – outside counsel firms or other vendors involved in or handling the matter.
- Open and close dates – important dates in matter timeline.
- Disposition – matter outcome.
- Financial – budget, internal, and external spend, invoices, credit notes, etc.

Consider the wealth of insights that can be discovered and questions that can be answered if just some of the data fields listed are collected and compared. For instance, when spend is increasing for a group of matters but there is no increase in case count, clients may question why and examine what's driving those costs. The same logic holds if the matter age is increasing, with regular billing, and no improvement in number of resolutions.

During the past two decades, I have worked with many large clients to analyze their data to understand what metrics can unveil and how those insights can be applied to improve performance, efficiency, and efficacy. It's always a lot of fun because you never know what you may uncover and it's a great reward to find an unexpected opportunity.

Financial reports that make cents (sense)

Financial reports are designed to evaluate financial management performance against a client's principled target. Examples include:

- Legal spend year over year;
- Budget compliance;
- Average case costs for select sets of like matters; and
- Released loss reserves.

Analytic reports such as the "Prior Year Average Cost per Matter Billed" and "Average Cost per Matters Closed (Life of Matter Costs)" reports compare the costs incurred on matters during the prior year with total costs for matters within the same segment of matters (here, by law firm). Such analyses use historical data to generate more credible budgets and projections, significantly improving both spend visibility and predictability. Sub-segmentation analyses (for example, by matter type and severity) provide further insight into likely future costs. Prior Year Average Cost per Matter Billed and Average Cost per Matters Closed are examples of good internal and external evaluations as well.

Year-End Performance against Client Budgets Analysis:

- Matters Billed.
- Net Fees.
- Net Expenses.
- Net Total Cost.
- Percentage of All Spend.
- Aggregating Percentage of All Spend.

Average Matter Cost for Pending Matters Analysis:

- Average Net Fees.
- Average Net Expenses.
- Average Total Cost.
- Matter Cost per Practice.

Average Matter Cost for Closed Matters:

- Average Net Fees.
- Average Net Expenses.
- Average Total Cost.
- Average Matter Cost Per Practice.

Managing finances and managing inventory are the key objectives of the legal department. The following reports evaluate the effectiveness of matter management efforts. The intent of these reports is to hold individuals, small groups, teams, and law firms accountable for inventory control. Examples include:

- Average Open Case Age.
- Average Closed Case Age.

- Closed To Received Ratio.
- Matters Closed Per Month by User.

Operations analysis and results

Now, let's look at some actual data our team analyzed and see what we can learn. Starting from the top, we began with Operations KPIs.

The purpose of this analysis for the client is normally two-fold. First, to identify which data fields are being populated within the matter management and eBilling systems and with how much integrity, from which meaningful metrics can be extracted. The second purpose is to attain a better understanding of firm billing practices such as how firms are assigning their resources with different levels of expertise and experiences. Clients never want to nickel-and-dime firms, they want to insist upon principled, consistent billing practices that provide quality efficiently.

Documenting and analyzing law firm invoice data helps to understand the aggregate and relative billing tendencies of one firm against another or against the group. The level of billing, the types of matters billed, the extent to which alternative fee arrangements are used, the types of resources billing, and the types of expenses billed were all examined to produce the following metrics and KPIs:

Billing information:

- Matter Types Billed.
- Matters Billed.
- Fees Billed.
- Expenses Billed.
- Fees by Timekeeper Role.
- Fees Billed Through AFAs.

Rate Information:

- Highest and Lowest Partner Rate.
- Highest and Lowest Associate Rate.
- Highest Paralegal Rate.
- Average Blended Rate.

Timekeeper Information:

- Highest Billed Rate by Timekeeper.
- Percentage of Eight Plus Hour Days Billed.
- Percentage of Days with Weekend and Holidays Billed.
- Task Code Tendencies.
- Unit Billing Tendencies.
- Timekeeper Billing with Different Rates.

Line Item Analysis By Timekeeper:

- Task Code Tendencies.
- Percentage of Time Billed per Task.
- Percentage of Time Billed per Activity.
- Block Billing Tendencies.
- Quality of Task Description.
- Duplicate Line Item Descriptions.

Now for some real results.

Rate changes over time

When looking at the average combined rates for each role individually and for all combined roles across the entire year, we see that rates are consistently being raised every quarter, which is quite unusual. This may seem

Role	Q1 (USD)	Q2 (USD)	Q3 (USD)	Q4 (USD)	Average (USD)
Partner	453	458	461	462	459
Associate	292	302	311	311	308
Paralegal	181	182	183	188	184
Legal assistant	114	119	121	122	119
Of counsel	251	255	257	266	259
Other	144	153	160	166	159
Blended average rate	261	263	268	269	265

to suggest that the firm has been increasing individuals' rates throughout the year, or timekeepers with higher rates were billing more often as the year went on. Another cause of the rate changes during the year could have been the frequent introduction of new lawyers on existing matters whose rates were often higher than the previous and existing lawyers.

Resource utilization

One of the things that clients analyze when evaluating how a particular firm handles matters is how resources are deployed for that project. This can be used to examine cost drivers across matter type but, even for similar matters or tasks, differences in how a firm chooses to assign resources can be analyzed and offer some telling insight. Resource utilization reports are derived from the firm's invoice line-item billing information and identify the timekeeper roles performing legal tasks by role as partner, associate, and so on. Using that information to compare against other firms performing similar tasks, legal ops teams can work with law firms to discuss opportunities for improving the utilization of resources properly. For instance, in the following table, this firm is assigning PA (partners) to perform 100 percent of the matter type of work, while other firms may also use other resources such as associate, paralegal, to reduce the burden and cost.

	Firm Allocation					Suggested Allocation				
	OC	PL	AS	PA	OT	OC	PL	AS	PA	OT
Matter				100%		7%	2%	44%	41%	6%
Litigation			15%	35%	50%	2%	8%	33%	30%	27%

Percent of time entries per unit billed

Take the table overleaf, analyzing the time entries by a firm to a client who requires billing in .10 increments:

You can see that several individuals billed in lump sum time units. There are a number of timekeepers who billed only in one-hour increments, which is unusual and suggests estimation. The analysis indicates that this is a widespread issue with this firm. Solace, Lee, Lopez, and Bozzeli billed 100 percent of all their time entries in one-hour increments. When we dug in and analyzed line-item descriptions, it quickly became obvious that those individuals billed one-hour for every meeting they attended or email they generated.

Chapter 7: Analyzing data to increase efficiencies – the client's perspective

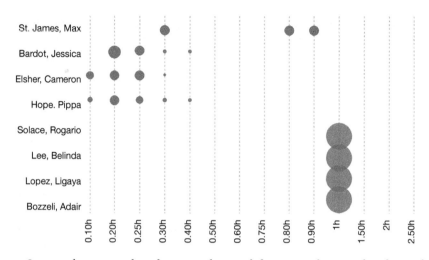

Separately, we analyzed time submitted for anomalies in the days of submission. The heatmap below shows the number of weekends and holidays for which time was billed, as well as heavy billing days (the days in which more than ten hours were billed).

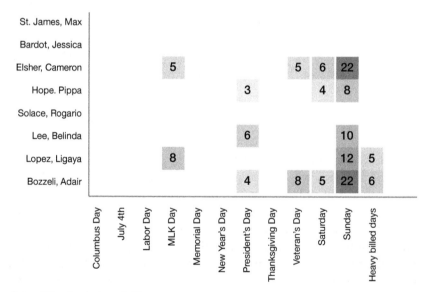

Repetitive task descriptions

Analysis of the frequency with which identical line-item descriptions of activity are submitted shows that often these duplicate descriptions reveal billing practices or repetitive tasks generated by inaccurate or automated entries that are billed without review to the client.

Timekeeper	Role	Description of Task	Number of Entries	Total fees (USD)
St. James, Max	Partner	Prepare for and attend plaintiff deposition	19	23,845
St. James, Max	Partner	Draft responsive leadings	14	10,340
Lopez, Ligaya	Paralegal	Attention to discovery correspondence	32	8,820

This occurrence is not uncommon, especially within a law firm handling repetitive work, but it can add up quickly. For instance, we noticed that for one firm, the deposition attendance entries came out to averaging more than 1,500 USD per deposition, which is odd, especially if outside counsel is performing the same deposition processes repeatedly, reducing preparation costs. Looking at the entries and reviewing a handful of line items will quickly alert the client to return the invoice to the firm for clarification.

Data quality

There are a lot of interesting insights we uncovered through this Operations KPI analysis using eBilling and ELM data. Clients wanted something that

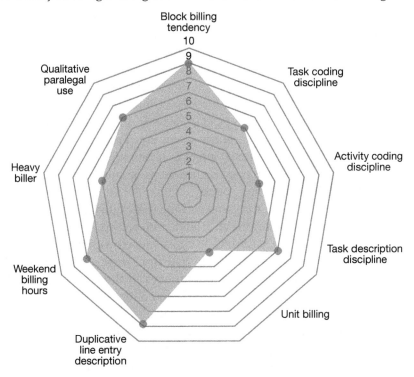

shows an aggregated, high-level look at overall law firm billing hygiene metrics. The metrics and ratings were partially data driven and partially the result of relative, qualitative impressions based on samplings of such things as the quality of UTBMS coding, line-item description quality, and the like. The chart on the previous page gave them an idea of data quality at a glance.

More advanced invoice data analytics

Most of the data we have been using so far comes from details tracked and submitted by firms to their clients. As part of each company's corporate policies, legal departments often have billing guidelines that list the invoice requirements and restrictions such as type of approved work and expenses, submission and rejection rules, deadlines and more. Clients use eBilling tools, outsourcing, and/or inhouse reviewers to make sure charges are compliant with the agreed billing guidelines. While some policies such as "we won't pay for online research" can be easily detected if coded correctly by eBilling tools, there are cases that require deeper knowledge of the specific services rendered, time invested, the level of expertise provided, and the type of extenuating circumstances of the matter in order to make approval decisions.

Having spent decades working with industry-leading corporate clients processing tens-of-thousands of invoices a year who were interested in leveraging emerging technology to detect anomalies charges, I wanted to answer their call. We carried out an in-depth research project to collect and train machine learning algorithms on detecting anomalous line-items in law firm invoices. We analyzed invoices for innumerable closed matters, to unmask patterns about the type of work being done in each phase, type or resources used, number of hours spent, etc. Then we finetuned and trained our models to eventually analyze incoming invoices, and with a decent accuracy highlight anomalous line-items beyond the ordinary capabilities of a traditional eBilling system.

For example, one of the analyses we did on these hundreds of thousands of line-items focused exclusively on UTBMS task coding. We used machine learning and some data modeling to teach our algorithms to crawl the invoice data and identify anomalies in how firms were assigning UTBMS codes to line items across all invoices throughout the matter history. We discovered occurrences of firms billing hours under L500, Appeal in the same invoice as L200, Pre-Trial Pleadings and Motions! In other instances, we saw firms using one or two codes as a catch-all, such as using L390 Other Discovery for 90 percent of discovery line items, instead of taking advantage of the other five specific and descriptive L300 Discovery codes.

This research and the result of the above project was conceived, led, and documented by the author and his team in a scientific paper, *Detecting Anomalous Invoice Line Items in the Legal Case Lifecycle* (2020)[1] which was accepted by the credited ICDM conference in 2021, for which the author also served as a chair.

References
1   https://arxiv.org/abs/2012.14511

Chapter 8:
Why your data might be useless

By Jaap Bosman, TGO Consulting

Type "antioxidants health benefits" in to Google and hit the search button, and within 0.6 seconds you get over 100 million hits. The internet and literature are awash with articles, studies, and reports that antioxidants are good for our health. Because of that, millions of people around the world include foods that contain high levels of antioxidants in their daily diet. That antioxidants are good is generally accepted by science.

A couple of years ago, a group of academics decided to review a large number of earlier studies into the effects of antioxidants. What they found shocked the academic community, as it appeared people who consume foods containing antioxidants on a regular basis have a healthier lifestyle than the average population. They do not just eat blueberries, but also less fat and refined sugars. They smoke less tobacco and drink less alcohol. They also tend to lead a more active lifestyle. When the researchers started taking into account the positive effects of the lifestyle of the people that consume antioxidants, what they found was that the antioxidants as such do not have a positive effect on our health. On the contrary, it proved that antioxidants could even be harmful...

This example is meant to illustrate that vast amounts of data are no guarantee that the results of the analysis will be valid. Numerous teams of academics had failed to recognize the healthy lifestyle bias that was distorting their data.

Snake oil

In November 2008, the until then relatively unknown English author Richard Susskind catapulted to fame as an international legal industry celebrity, with the publication of his book, *The End of Lawyers*.[1] Since then, Susskind has been invited to speak in over 40 countries and has addressed audiences (in person and electronically) numbering more than 250,000.

I think it is fair to say the book kicked off a virally growing Legal Tech frenzy. At some point there was a seminar or conference on Legal Tech in the main legal centers of the world every week. Countless articles have been written and many speakers have been making a living as prophets of technological disruption.

This also gave birth to a growing number of Legal Tech startups. I remember being present at a presentation in Amsterdam in the late 1990s where Mike Lynch, the founder of Autonomy, claimed that his software was "smarter than a human being". Autonomy was sold to US giant Hewlett Packard for $11bn in 2011. (Mike Lynch was later accused of fraud and prosecuted.)

Not surprisingly in this industry-wide excitement, law firms fell victim to Fear Of Missing Out (FOMO). Many CIOs were hastily appointed and law firm websites made bold statements on how advanced and forward-looking their IT strategy was. Law firms were en masse implementing advanced technology. At least that is what they claimed.

The reality is that most so-called technological revolutions never happen. In 2013, Google Glass was widely expected to be the next big thing. Today it is nothing more than a faint memory for some. Around the same time, in 2014, we were supposed to be at the beginning of a 3D-printing revolution. Most households would have 3D-printers at home and be their own manufacturers. Instead of buying and shipping physical goods, people would simply purchase a computer file and print whatever it was at home. Again, this "revolution" never took off. Self-driving cars? Not so much, or at least not yet.

Almost 15 years after *The End of Lawyers*, the Legal Tech hype seems to finally be coming to an end. The legal industry is moving from inflated expectations to sensible and gradual innovation. Today's legal tech is much more likely to be real medicine than the snake oil it was over more than a decade.

Data, an early experience
It must have been little over ten years ago, while I was still with a law firm. As a team, we frequently had to pitch for transactions. This regularly involved giving a fee quote. Fearing to lose the pitch because of the price, we always tried to come up with a competitive quote. After winning the mandate, despite all our experience, we often found that in the end we went way over budget and actually lost money. How frustrating.

At the time I was convinced that we could do better if only we could analyze the historical data from all the transactions we had done in the past. We decided to recruit a young and very smart econometrician who had graduated in data analytics to lead the project. Long story short: after a year or two we concluded that it would not work. It appeared that the time needed for a transaction could not be predicted using historical data. It was predominantly external factors that were not recorded that had a huge influence. Factors such as whether the client is a repeat player, or if the transaction is a once in a lifetime event. The size of the company, number of jurisdictions, industry, number of employees, ownership structure, etc. – all these are obviously known at the time the transaction is done, but they are not recorded in the system so they cannot be used for analysis later on.

For me, this was a super interesting and valuable experience. Not only did I learn a lot about data analytics (I did my first Monte Carlo Simulation, for example), I also realized that availability, quality, and quantity of the dataset is crucial for any project to succeed. This is still the prime reason why Artificial Intelligence and Data Analytics projects fail. Often the focus is on the clever algorithm, but in reality this is seldom the problem. The challenge is in the data. This includes both the data used for the analysis and the data used to train the algorithm.

25 percent savings on external legal spend

If one would ask clients what they would want their law firms to improve upon, the most common answer would likely be price. For over a decade, clients have been complaining that law firms are too expensive. But are they?

In 2018, my team and I carried out a large-scale analysis of real-world billing and time-keeping data from a number of very large companies that buy for millions external legal services annually. The dataset we analyzed contained almost a million records of anonymized individual timekeepers from a large number of anonymized law firms. What we found was a big surprise for everyone – about 25 percent of all the billable time that lawyers charge for is caused by preventable inefficiencies on the clients' side!

Please let this sink in for a moment. If clients would be more efficient in managing the relationship with their outside counsel, they would save 25 percent without negotiating lower rates. The only thing clients need to do is make sure they prepare all the documents and information the lawyer will need and provide it in a well-organized, accessible manner. Clients should not change the scope of work and should create a clear and efficient communication and decision-taking structure.

I think every client would agree that it does not make sense to pay a premium to a lawyer for sorting out information and for acting as a communication intermediary between different departments and people in the client's own organization. If the client's legal department would be understaffed and short on resources, hiring a temporary paralegal would come at a fraction of the cost. The problem is that clients are not aware of this opportunity.

For me, this is a great example of the power and benefits of employing data analytics in the legal industry. Not only because we did it and found this revolutionary insight, but because, if used properly, data analytics can be a most powerful management tool. Before taking decisions it is best to know all the relevant facts. I'm not saying data should drive the decision. Some of the best decisions are based on intuition, but even gut-feeling needs to be fueled by facts. When it comes to the legal industry, there is still a tremendous amount of room for improvement as it comes to the use of data and data-analytics.

CRM frustrations

The legal industry could greatly benefit from employing some proper data analytics. In order to be able to start doing that, law firms first need clean data. While this might sound easy, it is far easier said than done. Let look at a CRM database as an example.

Typically, law firms go through a five-year cycle of implementing a new CRM system. This is far more frequent than their financial systems, for instance, which are known to be used for a decade or more. This, despite the financial system being of much more vital importance to the business. So, why are law firms en masse throwing money at their CRM tools?

The main reason behind the short lifecycle of a CRM system is not that the software is outdated and/or no longer supported. It is also not that the current software is too restricted in its possibilities. No, the software as such is just fine.

So, if the software is just fine and capable, how come law firms still want to spend vast sums of money on the next system, which might look a bit different, but will basically be the same? For the record, unless your firm has in excess of 5,000 or so contacts, Microsoft Excel will probably also do just fine.

The need to change is mainly driven by frustration regarding the data. Partners feel frustrated their CRM system is unreliable and does not contain all the information they want. CRM data invariably contains doublures, contacts who moved to another employer, retired, or got fired. Some contacts may even no longer be alive. If a newsletter or – even worse – an invitation is sent to such a contact, partners get frustrated and sometimes infuriated. Clearly this has nothing to do with the software, it is only a matter of data. The data in the system is not clean and uncleaned data is mostly useless.

Not only do partners feel frustrated if they come across contacts that are outdated, they also are expecting the CRM system to pull up all contacts that meet certain criteria. This could be all contacts who are at C-suite level, or all contacts that have an interest in a certain topic. Most of the time this type of information is not in the system. Not all CEOs, for example, are created equal. Perhaps you do not want the CEO of a small regional family business to sit alongside the CEO of a large, listed company. Unfortunately, company size is not an adequate tool for determining which are the high level CEOs. A private equity company that invests billions and owns a stake in large companies might be rather small itself.

The same goes for interests in certain topics. Let's say the firm is planning to organize a seminar on the latest developments in renewable energy. Should it just invite contacts from the energy industry, or also investors? The problem with investors is that they are classified as "financial" and not as "energy". Both the C-suite and the "area of interest" example are about the richness of the data. Here the data is correct, but – from the perspective of the need – incomplete.

When partners demand a new CRM system, they are actually blaming the system for not containing the right data. If is, however, not the system at fault. The root cause is the data. That is why a new system is never the solution. That is why, after five years or so, the whole cycle starts again. Much to the benefit of the suppliers of CRM software.

Financial analysis – risks and shortcomings

While the financial systems of law firms remain around for much longer than their CRM systems, that does not mean that the data it contains is much better. Finance software is primarily geared towards sending invoices and doing basic bookkeeping.

For both objectives these systems work just fine. The financial system contains matter numbers, a billing address, and time spent per individual fee-earner, and a provision for special fee arrangements. This is enough to send out invoices and for this purpose the data is reliable.

The data being reliable and usable for the purpose of billing, does, however, not imply that the data is also usable for further financial analysis. In my practice, we do a lot of what we call Financial Business Analysis©, and we have over the years experienced first-hand how unsuited data straight from the financial system could be for this purpose.

When using the billing data for further analysis, the first problem you will come across is that of the "billing partner". The partner in whose name the file is may or may not be the partner that has actually been responsible for client and matter management in a particular file. When you want to make an analysis of revenue per partner and utilization ratios, this is a huge obstacle.

Secondly, the client, according to the invoice, may or may not be the actual client. Both private equity and insurance clients often prefer to have the invoices in the name of the target, respectively the insured party. This will obviously obstruct a clear view on the total revenue of such client. It is also not uncommon that a client consists of a group of companies, some of which may have "obscure" names. Among these are special purpose companies. If such companies are not connected to the mother company in the financial system, their revenue will be missed in the analysis of what are the best clients of the firm, a practice group, or a partner.

These are just some examples of data that, if used straight out of the system, will inevitably lead to invalid conclusion in the analysis. We see this happen a lot. Mostly, law firms just assume the financial data can be used without further scrutiny. Many financial software suites even offer analytical tools based on the data in the system. There is never a clear warning that the analysis will probably be unsuited for management purposes.

Much of the data is "useless"
Just as with the CRM system, it is not the software that is to blame, it is the integrity of the data. The grim reality is that much of the data that law firms hold is in principle useless. It is not just contact data or financial data. It is potentially all data. Take your document management system. In theory, it would only contain one version of each document, so everyone would always have access to the latest version. In reality, documents get stored in private folders and multiple slightly different versions will exist at the same time in different places. The same document can also be stored under different names, making it hard or even impossible to know for sure which version to use.

The red thread so far is that humans are the weakest link as it comes to data. People are lazy or pressed for time and don't put the correct information in the CRM system. I know an employment partner at a prestigious law firm who once helped to terminate the contract of a high profile CEO. Given the extremely sensitive nature, the whole process was wrapped in the greatest secrecy. Months later this partner ignited in rage when it turned out the ousted CEO had been sent an invitation for one of the firm's boardroom events. It should have been his responsibility to update the CRM system, but being a high profile partner, he could not be bothered by such a mundane triviality. The problem is that CRM systems still are not clairvoyant.

Not updating the data is one problem, not understanding the data is another. Most lawyers are not great with numbers. There is a reason why back at college they did not opt to pursue a career in the beta-sciences. There is no reason why managing partners would be an exception. It still amazes me how law firm leaders accept the results of financial analysis without any scrutiny of the nature of the data used. This would never happen if it were not numerical. Anything verbal would invariably be challenged.

Data analysis for law firms
Law firms are sitting on a treasure trove of data, but it is not what they think. Like I did myself over a decade ago, law firms are still trying to use historical data for pricing purposes. Some larger law firms even have pricing professionals or a dedicated pricing team to help partners get mandates and clients while not losing money at the same time. The fact is that not only do law firms still not keep records of the relevant data that is needed to accurately predict the time spent by level of experience (this was my conclusion back in 2009 and it still holds true), but they also vastly underestimate how much – clean – data is needed to make a valid analysis. Much more than most law firms would have.

If the potential is not in analyzing historical data for pricing purposes, where is it? The answer is in the financial records of the firm. All law firms have a professional financial department that makes sure all billable hours get invoiced and paid. From an accounting perspective, the finance departments are extremely well organized. All time that has been entered in the timesheets will show up in an invoice to the client (subject to the partner's approval of course).

An accounting and billing machine is very different in organization, skills, and mentality from a management-data analytics department. There are lots of opportunities in analyzing the data that underlies the accounting. We have developed a method that we branded Financial Business Analysis© and without exception this provides surprising new insights to law firm management. This is not rocket science and, after we show them how to do it, any law firm can do it on their own. By applying Financial Business Analysis© law firms, on average, improve their bottom line by five to ten percent, which makes a strong business case for analyzing those data.

Prediction and prevention

Companies don't have legal issues, they have a business to run. Ideally a company would like to avoid legal issues altogether. That is why most SMEs try to avoid disputes involving lawyers at all costs. Actually, this is not unlike medical issues. No one wants to be ill, people in general will want to avoid doctors and hospitals. The difference is that the medical profession recognized this decades ago and started to focus on prevention and prediction.

It would be very unsatisfying if doctors would only cure people who are already ill. That is why there has been a lot of public and private research trying to figure out why people get sick and what can be done to prevent this from happening. By now we all know that smoking might cause tumors and that lead plumbing for tap water could seriously affect the development of the brain and nervous system of children.

Why is this relevant for the legal industry? The surprising thing is that lawyers have never focused on prevention and prediction. When I went to law school, like all of you, I had to study lots of case law. As a consequence, lawyers are focused on the outcome of a dispute and not on why disputes arise in the first place.

Police forces are already experimenting with Artificial Intelligence-based tools that help predict where crimes might happen. This will help the police department to locate resources and might even help prevent crimes from happening. Given the early stages, none of this is perfect, but some results look promising.

If data analytics can help prevent a highly individual thing as crime, it certainly must have the potential to help prevent commercial disputes. Academic studies show that there are certain underlying patterns that can help predict what will happen next. For society it often starts with discussions on social media, followed by discussions on major news platforms. This in turn leads to discussions in politics, leading to legislation. Legislation, after a while, will lead to enforcement. By studying and analyzing what is trending on social media today, companies could anticipate tomorrow's legislation and enforcement. There are many yet untapped opportunities for the legal industry to apply all sorts of data analytics for prediction and prevention of disputes (or PR disasters).

Data are the alpha and the omega

This chapter is about the use of data analytics in the legal industry. As you have seen, there are many very useful opportunities waiting to be explored. Data analytics can help companies save substantially on their external legal spend. It can help prevent disputes and public opinion catastrophes. Data analytics can help law firms to better manage their business and significantly boost their bottom line. These are just examples, and there are many more opportunities waiting to be unlocked. Data can be a goldmine for the legal sector.

If I say it can be a gold mine, then that is on purpose. There are two crucial conditions that must be met for data to be useful for analysis, delivering meaningful results. Condition number one is that the data must be clean and unbiased. This condition is already very hard to meet. The second condition is that you need a huge amount of clean and unbiased data for drawing valid conclusions. If there is not enough data the results will be unreliable at best.

Don't let this put you off. Just be aware that you will need to calculate for spending a lot of time and effort on cleaning the data before you can start. But it would be fair to say that data analytics will become an essential tool for the legal industry in the years to come. Those who start today will definitely have a competitive advantage.

References
1   Richard Susskind, *The End of Lawyers? Rethinking the Nature of Legal Services*, Oxford University Press), Oxford, 2008.

Chapter 9:
Data in the 2020s

By Paul Brook, Dell Technologies

The 2020s will be defined by data. Global companies, household names such as Apple, Amazon, Meta (Facebook), and Google, are all creating and consuming huge volumes of data whilst at the same time using it to create new and improved business outcomes. Data is being used to drive efficiencies in business and in governments, it is being curated into scientific and artistic discovery, new knowledge, and intellectual property; data is being turned into Money.

What do you know about data? Maybe you have read a lot about it, have seen documentaries about it, maybe you use data all the time, maybe you are thinking you know enough about data to last a lifetime, maybe you don't really care too much what you know. All views are welcome, but one point is worth making – Data is very important, and it should matter very much to you. Sharp eyes will have noticed how Data has just gained a capital D. This is because I am going to argue that Data is a thing. It has value, it is monetized, it has capital value. Data is not only a descriptive term used by computer geeks, but also part of the topics regularly on main board discussions. It is both a business resource and a business tool. Increasingly, it is viewed as being mission critical.

This chapter is going to enquire further into this "top table" discussion. To be able to fully appreciate how Data gets to be at this level we will start this section with a few short examples of how Data got into the "big league" of topics for so many organisations. Then, we turn our attention to some of the Data-driven topics that I believe will dominate the rest of this decade. We'll look at the hot topics, the "need to know", followed by areas where the Data topic has become business as usual (where you still need to know about it but the topic is one that is no longer hot). In a sub-set of this section, I will suggest a couple of areas where the Data race has already been run. The final part stares into the key Data issues that I believe will create both threats and high opportunity for the legal profession; indeed, for many professional services. For example, by the time

Chapter 9: Data in the 2020s

the Data Decade ends, digital twins will be business as usual. Finally, of course, a summary and a couple of suggestions for either further research or personal comment. Expect an extremely hopeful conclusion.

Data at the top table

Data has a capital and is a top-table discussion. When did this happen? Did I miss the meeting? Data entered the mainstream business/organisational culture by stealth whilst, at the same time, it rode into the room with the subtlety of a circus parade. Of course, Data is not a new thing; for years, organisations have "run the numbers". Sam Walton, founder of the Walmart retail chain, was famously said to be obsessed with the numbers. He was often remembered for carrying a yellow legal pad around with him, on which he went through the numbers with his managers. Honestly, not unusual behaviour for a business leader. But Data is not just numbers. Maybe this is where the "old" world view gets stuck. For many organisations the numbers were the data. In the Data decade, numbers matter, but Data covers so much more than a spreadsheet or a corporate estimate. Data floods in from a myriad of places and from an increasingly large number of things. This creates patterns, it leaves watermarks, and it points toward possibilities. Past, present, and future can be observed in Data patterns. What we now need to look at is a few examples of just how Data is being used today in the consumer market, in government, and in the B2B (business to business) world.

Data examples

One of the world-famous Data-driven companies is Amazon. Amazon understood the value of Data from the outset of its business. It used it to support growing its business whilst seeking to ensure that Data helped make the customer experience the best it could be. Take a moment to look at the early career of Jeff Bezos, the founder of Amazon. Starting at a Fintech telecoms start-up, on into the banking industry and then a hedge fund (he made senior VP there at the age of 30), Bezos seems to have cut his teeth in the world of numbers. Taking this into the online world, you are probably all familiar with the "Amazon classic" "people who bought this also looked at this" feature. This is a classic upsell though product recommendation, a common technique, but Amazon differentiated through one important thing. Whilst competitors had editors and product managers creating these recommendations, early on Amazon turned to a technology called the recommendation engine. This takes real-world behaviours collected from real systems; for example, collecting information about what millions of customers *really* bought next, and builds this into a personalized suggestion.

Back in 2013, I was citing a report[1] suggesting up to 25 percent of Amazon's revenue (at the time this was around $34bn) was being generated from suggestions made by the recommendation engine. I have since heard this could have been as much as 35 percent. More than ten years ago, Amazon was said to be automating the sales of between a quarter to a third of turnover. Just think what might be possible today. Back in 2012, some "tables" had Amazon in the world's top ten retailers, whilst others put them at number two globally (just behind Walmart).[2] So, a massive organisation was using Data to generate a sizable portion of its turnover. Trust me, the founder of Walmart baked into his company a strong Data culture. Whilst I don't have the detail, be sure that they too will have some fascinating examples of Data contributing to their bottom line. Now you might be thinking the legal profession is not the same as a grocer. Hold that thought, as the lessons might not be about the what, so much as the how.

Play a game now. Imagine I had asked you in 2012 to create a web page/portal that could be instantly shown to over 200 million people and each one of them would receive "home page" experience based upon what they had viewed previously. 200-million unique, instant personalized pages. You would have laughed at me. Today this is exactly what Netflix does, and you don't even notice until you see another Netflix subscriber's "home" page. Data is being increasingly used, harvested at source from customers' own systems, interactions with sites and purchases (websites and "real" shopping) and then used to create highly personalized offers to that customer. Data is turned into cash. Data is being used to bring a hugely beneficial customer experience to both the consumer market and the huge B2B sector. That customer experience translates directly into revenue and margin for many organisations. Data is being used to make customers happier, therefore likely to spend more with that organisation that makes them happy. In the public sector this translates into lower cost, greater accuracy, and therefore often much-improved efficiency. Put simply, dealing with the government becomes easier. For the public sector, it means citizens are just a little bit less frustrated with the daily business of government administration. That makes government more popular, or certainly less disparaged, and is likely to manifest as reduced cost. Using Data to improve the customer, or citizen, experience; this is the hot topic.

You will probably now think about what your organisation has in common with Netflix and Amazon. Born as internet companies I am

Chapter 9: Data in the 2020s

guessing that you feel I am throwing a ball in the wrong direction. You will expect that Netflix and Amazon have Data, heaps of it. And, of course, you expect that they would monetise the Data they create; both Netflix and Amazon could easily be seen as Data factories, which have no history outside of the digital world and the internet age. Yep. You have spotted that it is too easy to flag Data as being vital to businesses that were created to take advantage of a medium that is fundamentally digital by design and data-centric by default. So, to pivot towards an area that is still a hot topic, but is also becoming business as usual, we will look at maintaining railway trains and associated rolling stock. This industry, rather than being born on the internet, is a few hundred years old.

A few years ago, I met with a company that manufactured, maintained, and repaired wheels used on trains and railway rolling stock. In case you are not sure, rolling stock is likely to be exactly what you think it is – carriages for passengers and wagons for freight and goods. Basically, the railway's "stock" of things that roll; differentiated from stock of things that move under power. Why not "pulling stock"? Because sometimes these things are pushed. So now you are a railway expert. You would expect that folks who make wheels for trains and rolling stock to be technical folks by the nature of the work. You would expect the classic engineering bias within such an organisation. You would be right in your expectation. They know they produce a product that will be operating in harsh conditions. It will be subject to stresses and strains. It will be subjected to a regular usage that inflicts a heavy wear and tear toll upon the product. The manufacturing process is well understood and well governed. The general usage and associated wear and tear upon the product are well recognised and the process for maintenance and repair over time is well understood. Yes, some data is used but what more can possibly be done to help this engineering led, traditional industry? The answer: a lot.

A group often associated with a close understanding of Data is the scientific and engineering communities. These are of course the very sort of folk who are engaged in the design, manufacture, and maintenance of wheels for trains and railway rolling stock. They understand that differing operating temperatures impact the performance and life span of their product. They understand how manufacturing flaws, even at microscopic level, impact the operation life of the product. They understand maintenance routines, production recipes, load, and so on and so forth. They are experts. They recognise how the gathering of Data about the production, maintenance, and the daily workings of each wheel can have a significant value to the lifespan and performance of these products. A company in the US called

Duos Technologies Group (Nasdaq: DUOT)[3] use an AI-based technology and some very "real world" technology in a product they call RIP or Railcar Inspection Portal. This is not just for wheels. The RIP product uses sensor equipment and AI technologies to provide Data against which "rolling stock" is inspected for status. This is done securely and remotely, whilst the train is moving at full speed. Technology that saves time, therefore saves money. In addition, safety is improved as the quality and reliability of regular inspection (with associated action taken when an issue is spotted) has a direct impact upon safety records.

Data is used by sports teams, by stadium officials, by the streaming and broadcast companies, by the advertisers sponsoring the sport, or filling ad breaks in-between the event. The world of energy generation and distribution uses Data to predict energy use and support long-term planning; they even use AI to make sure that vegetation growing underneath power cables is kept under control though effective inspection. The same industries use Data to support energy reduction, a business acting to reduce consumption of its product, but here Data can help support a sustainable future. Scientists, engineers, creatives, advertisers, manufacturers, artisans and entrepreneurs, charities, and governments all pack Data into their daily business. I have met businesses that use Data to prevent potentially horrific incidents. The future of counter terrorism may indeed have a huge element of Data collection. But in truth when did this ever not be the case? Data has played a part in so many things. Medical scientists and researchers who seek cures, vaccines, and drug discovery all create, use, collect, and store Data volumes that stagger the mind. Data is embedded as much in the traditional industries such as the railroad/train industry as it is in the internet defined businesses that are now household names. Data is everywhere and it is being used in places you would never guess. Data is a thing.

Hot or not?
Some of these Data-driven industrial and not-for-profit use cases, the inventions, and discoveries, have become so ubiquitous that the technical race is over – the winner might not be decided but the core of the runners are already racing. Some are now even becoming rather dated. The Data universe is an unforgiving place. Darwinian at best; fail to make headway and you are done. Having a view on these patterns matters as much as backing the wrong horse in a race. It could lose you your shirt. This section reviews the "what's hot and what's not" side of Data. The context is with an eye to what is likely to be important within the legal, and associated

sectors. This is not going to predict winners and losers; instead, this provides a general view of themes that might recur or continue to extend and others that are likely to wither away.

Easier to start with the likely to wither away. Some of the early Data players and early front runners focused time and effort upon simply doing the same stuff we have always done except delivering the results in a shorter space of time. Much of the Data-driven B2B market focused upon this. My take is very much along the lines of Henry Ford's famous line about people knowing what they want; he suggested they would have asked for faster horses. Much of the early Data world was obsessed with speed. Speed, or velocity, is of course important to many organisations; however, for many, that race is won. Today, accelerating the speed of Data is a vanity project. The race for my Data is faster than your Data is over except in a few lucrative but otherwise niche business situations. Honestly. I have seen technology "white papers" (the term comes from the days where government documents were printed on different colours of paper – white papers were intended for public distribution) talk about latency as low as four milliseconds or lower. If you even know what that means it demonstrates the craziness of any speed debate. I am not dismissing latency (for the technology minded) but what I am suggesting is when these units of measurement are described in publicly available technology papers then the speed of Data is done. Point to be made: Every day has more than 86 million milliseconds. Time is money, but for other than a small section of niche businesses and use-cases, Data speed is over. It will get faster and therefore we will cram more Data into ever decreasingly small segments of time. But pure speed – over and done. Anyone comes to you with a product or a proposition that boasts "fastest, quickest, lowest latency" – whatever the expression used to denote "quickest" – then find somebody informed in the matter and beware. It is likely you are betting on a race that is already run.

So, if not speed then what? Areas that seem to be taking the world by storm are where Data from multiple sources is combined. Early winners proved that taking a lot of Data, and a lot of data means on a scale almost unimaginable, taking this from multiple sources, and using the "natural" speed of technology to predict, for example, what folks might buy next, what adverts to show them or what websites/apps these folks might visit next. These Data giants made a very effective business case for both the velocity and volume of data; they proved that using multiple types and sources often enriched the Data and made some interesting conclusions and patterns become apparent. You know who these folks are. They are

Google (parent company Alphabet), Facebook (now META), Uber and many other darlings of the Silicon Valley Venture Capital community.

A huge area of investment in the business world, and increasingly extending into the public sector, is that of the Customer (or Citizen) experience. The amazing and almost unbelievable discovery made by modern business is that if you make it easy for people to do business with you – or for a citizen to interact with you – the theory goes you will profit by this with larger sales, larger numbers of sales, and likely a lower cost of sales, thereby likely higher margin on sales. Government like the lower cost but some governments really like the interaction such a citizen experience can create, as this interaction is an opportunity for monitoring. You are probably able to spot the sarcastic tone; for I am sure that if we were able to sit in a Phoenician market some thousand years before the common era (One thousand BC in old money) the traders would all be looking at reducing friction between buyer and seller. Making it easy to do business with them. This would have been how some of the early economic basics were established. Back then, innovations included keeping stock, having warehouses, efficient ports for ships. All of these (then) amazing innovations were designed to make the customer experience with a Phoenician trader way easier than with a competitor from another part of the cradle of civilization.

Nothing new under the sun they say; however, these modern levels of Data, both the volume and the detail, allow something extremely interesting to happen. Super-high grade, or fine-grained inspection, together with system, herd, or crowd-level behaviours. And the internet crowds are huge, vast swells of both humanity and machines. When folks playing computer games average every month in the 100+ million, when a streaming entertainment service can have 300 million customers, then it is reasonable to assume they use intelligent software and machines to analyse what subscribers are doing. Very reasonable to assume this. This is the scale where machine learning/Artificial Intelligence (AI) starts to become essential. It is very easy to see why a personalised service for 300 million folks requires heavy levels of machine/software intervention. It is harder to see how such automation is even desired in a business where far smaller numbers of customers are using the services.

In fact, it is easy to assume that only the consumer world of high-volume customer interaction makes any sense for AI. This is a mistake. AI and the associated benefits it can bring across a wide range of business areas are a hot topic; they include terms such as "automation" and "frictionless". Sounds like consultancy speak. But the legal profession, just as many other professional and/or expert services, is going to be running hard to keep up with automation. Take the examples of AI used in clinical and medical environments, such as in the field of pathology. AIs can deliver an accuracy of diagnosis equal to, and sometime superior to, a well-trained human pathologist. Is this going to end work and employment for pathology practitioners? Absolutely not; demand outstrips supply for sure and many factors mean the AI assisted diagnosis is going to become an expected medical practice. This expectation adds further complexity to the already complex legal world of medical practice and care; however, I anticipate a time when a newly qualified pathologist automatically expects to work with an AI assistant.

Threats and opportunities
Many will read this with a certain disbelief, but it is essential to understand that these systems not only exist today but are being used increasingly across the medical and clinical world. Automating elements of these services is already happening. It means increased numbers of people have access to these medical services, it means patient treatment improves and, in many cases, lives are saved as restrictions in supply become reduced, particularly the supply of professionally qualified people. Scale becomes more possible when access becomes easier. Cost barriers reduce. Do not be afraid of AI and the automation it brings. Embrace it, as this is one area where professional services can fix the scaling issue. The scaling issue of the limits of either expertise or time any one person, or one fee earner, might have.

The challenging statement here is very much that of the term "scaling issue". The legal, medical, accounting, indeed any form of professional services, are limited by the number of qualified or skilled people able to efficiently do the thing they need to do. For the legal profession this might include many disciplines within the wide body of legal practice. The limitation is that, within reason, if you cannot find a person, or persons with sufficient expertise, then the activity you need undertaking simply cannot get done. I am sure it is reasonable to suggest that work cannot be billed if it cannot be done. If work undertaken is incomplete or below standard, the cost often far outweighs any short-term monetary gain. Scale in the professional services and indeed in any people-based business is limited because of a lack of qualified, capable, or willing people. This is the scaling issue and AI can help fix this.

We surely all agree that it is not easy to find suitably qualified, experienced, and willing people able to perform professional (chargeable) work. The restricted "talent pool" is a limiter upon the potential total amount of professional billable work that the firm, practice, or organisation, can carry out. Now imagine if an effective digital twin of a legal professional could be created. Maybe a twin that is like the highly effective pathology AI. This could extend effective working time (time that could be billable) to a level that is potentially infinite. Hold that thought and turn your mind to the Amazon sales process. Pre-internet, the old ways of selling "like Amazon" was not only via retail; sales were often also though telephone and mail order. Catalogue sales were big business. Businesses generated sales by way of direct posted mailings, paper flyers, adverts in newspapers, magazines etc. Again, limited by the people at the back of the process taking the customer order, an order that may arrive in hundreds of different formats, re-entering these into the company's own systems and moving the request for goods into the next stage of the process. All of this worked, but it was a very manual process and processing each sale came at a high fixed cost, even if a customer was repeatedly ordering the same or similar products. Amazon has reduced many of these initial costs to a level that is close to zero. This is not suggesting that it costs nothing to run Amazon; this is stating that the acquisition cost of one additional sale is virtually zero. This is the power of Digital; this is where skilled automation creates opportunities that make the mind boggle.

In asking you to imagine an infinitely billable, relatively low cost, digital twin, I hope that you started to think about where this could go in all professional service, not just the legal profession. A digital twin can be many things. Industry has for years created simulations of things that were then sent on for manufacturing. Cars have been digitally crashed-tested for a long time now – this is one of the reasons so many variations of car models can be produced. The real-world physics of a car crashing is well understood, and the simulation is an incredibly accurate prediction of a "real world" version of such a crash. Whilst this simulated crash-test could be described as a digital twin, the term suggests so much more. Increasingly, we are seeing digital twins of entire factories, designed to help optimise and automate high-quality production standards. We see digital twins for medical purposes. I have talked with people who are developing a digital twin of an individual cancer cell – using this twin to test what combination of medical interventions are most effective. Complex digital twins of an individual person are a way off, but I have seen realistic digitally rendered people, animations that are highly realistic. These use AI to respond to the frequently asked questions that normally cost call centres so much money to process manually by call centre staff. This digital twin can answer an incoming enquiry, on a video link, mimic an effective human interaction, in multiple languages, for no pay, 24 hours a day, every day of the year. Now imagine having this service in a legal context. Indeed, in almost any remote human interaction.

Two things are likely to be happening now; you are either laughing about the craziness of the proposal for a "fake, digital, cartoon" legal professional, thinking how this section is going too far. This reaction is not uncommon. The alternative is that you are starting to think about what a legal business, or indeed what any professional services organisation, could potentially do with technology such as this; reach more people, lower costs, improve quality, maybe filter out timewasters but promote quality enquiries, thus reducing new business acquisition costs. Offer high levels of legal advice but in a virtual way. Deliver services in multiple languages, multiple legal frameworks, and do all this 24 hours a day every day of the year. You may think this all to be impossible but consider this: human beings cannot fly, yet I am guessing every reader would say that you have indeed flown, many of you flown many times over great distances. OK, I am playing with words. The plane flies and you are a passenger. A machine was invented, developed, and continues to be used to do something humans cannot do. The machine means we fly. Now a digital professional twin could be such a machine that allows people-based services businesses to soar and to scale.

A digital twin is basically software code, hardware to run software and Data. Sure, some creativity might be involved in the modelling of the images used. You may model the twin upon a real place, thing, or person. The office that the twin appears to be working from might be a digital twin of a real office, or it could have been designed from scratch as a virtual image. Somebody, more likely many somebodies, will own the infrastructure, code, and the Data with which the code interacts to create the functional digital twin. You may have heard people say: "Learn how to code", suggesting that being able to create or write computer software code is a brilliant thing. Indeed, it is. But I heard a UK-based businessperson at an industry event suggesting that the truly entrepreneurial mind thinks "How can I employ people who know how to code" and get these people to code stuff that people want to use, buy, trade, or otherwise engage with.

You will also have heard that "Data is the new Oil". No arguments from me or indeed from many folks today. So, these two well-worn technology gems point to a very interesting conclusion. Own the code and own the Data; in a digital world these are the core means of production. You maybe want to own a heap of other things but the core code and Data? Own it and leave this matter in no doubt. Then run the numbers of a business that does not yet exist. Run the numbers for the cost of developing and running a legal digital twin, the revenue this twin could earn minus the costs of maintaining the twin – and maintaining includes feeding with Data (remember about mixing Data at scale) and watering with code updates. Also, maintaining means the AI needs to be calibrated to events that change in the real world. (This is known as inferencing.) All costs. Then figure out how many possible new fee-paying customers this twin could deal with. Then create it. Now, I am not a genius, but if I think this is possible, many smart people are likely already doing something very similar to this but with disruptive intent.

Do you think that "Big Data" has faded away? The ten or so years starting around 2008 were what we can identify as the Data evangelist era. The phrase "Data is the new oil" littered the technology and business community, heard across the world at conferences, trade shows, press, blogs, and so forth. June 2011 saw the McKinsey Global Institute publish its hugely influential "Big Data: The next frontier for innovation, competition and productivity".[4] The world had already seen companies using data to create new business and grow existing business; many of the organisations were adopting the California Bay Area mentality of using Data to model a customer experience. Data pointed toward new and efficient revenue generation. Start-ups, where Data was seen as a key resource to be mined, became a well-trodden path against which billions of dollars of Venture Capital and other investment funding were being made. Today it is not unreasonable to ask where all this noise has gone. Was this a bubble that burst or was it a hype that faded away? The answer is absolutely neither of these. The truth is that incorporating the "Data Science" and associated "Big Data" methodologies into regular business and public sector organisations has become very much business as usual.

Very much as McKinsey predicted, organisations that embraced Big Data, and adopted a Data-driven approach, seem to have grown and thrived. They have become more efficient and productive. Organisations that chose not to adopt Big Data, or who were slow or late in adopting Data-driven practices, found they often experienced stagnant or even shrinking revenues and operations. Through automation, often involving AI, or through rapid customer/partner/operational and supply chain interactions, the software and hardware, clouds and networks, all come together in the world today to continue our journey into a highly digitised world. This is important because a highly digitised world, by the nature of digital, will create a lot of Data. The result is that Big Data is now simply called Data. The next few years are going to see an increase in Data and automation due to something that is already happening; that thing is 5G.

What exactly is 5G? UK communications regulator OFCOM defines 5G as being the new generation of wireless technology. From my point of view this is a raw definition. Factually accurate but of little practical value. Now I do urge you to look up 5G on the Ofcom website,[5] as whilst the definition of 5G seems a little basic, the site goes on to describe the potential impact that 5G may have on our lives. As with so many technology innovations, some of the predictions and proposals are speculative; however, the site describes current features that, when coupled with 5G, become a new network of things and people that interact with other things and people all the time. A very simple example: your car may, with 5G technology, simply refuse to "skip" a red traffic light. The car driving behind you may refuse to run into the back of you. I have a car, a well-known brand and one that rarely gets described as premium, fitted with sensors at the front of the car and with software and advanced safety features that will apply the brakes if the car senses a stationary/fixed object in front of it whilst the car is in motion.

I have experienced this emergency autobrake at first hand. It prevented an accident. The car reacted far quicker and with greater efficiency than I did. Now with 5G, the prediction is that not only would the car I drive "sense" the stationary vehicle in front of me, but the stationary vehicle would have "transmitted" its status to my car in advance of my turning the corner. No emergency braking incident would have been required as the connected vehicles would already have been managing and anticipating the safety of the situation. That is an area where 5G could take existing technology and provide an enhanced safety experience.

We would expect that both vehicles would use 5G to transmit Data to whatever organisation has agreed to receive this Data or is legally required to receive such information. 5G and AI based automation may simply mean many accidents do not happen in the first place. The end is in sight for those "Have you been involved in an accident" type of calls we so often get, but as one business opportunity closes another opportunity opens. What is the legal status of a vehicle whose safety or 5G information features have been removed or tampered with? Maybe this is a legal service that can be highly automated. You could make a bunch of money informing vehicles to steer clear of hand driven vehicles or even steer clear of people with poor safety records or who carry several speeding tickets. A legal service where a subscriber pays to avoid situations that have the potential to require legal involvement – how would that ever work? Surely in fact that is a mainstay of the legal profession. Clients on retainer already do receive advice that includes how to avoid legal problems. So, a 5G connected vehicle that is provided with practical (automated) service about possible problem avoidance might be a viable business opportunity.

The advent of 5G is very much about things being connected to other things. The example of the vehicle being connected to the other vehicle is a very common illustration of 5G, but it goes further. Staying with the driving theme, imagine a "smart road" where road signs giving lane and safety advice communicate with the car. The road sign will be "talking" with your car about, for example, a lane being blocked, or a general hazard, and your vehicle will manoeuvre into another lane (when it is safe to do so). Traffic lights will talk to your car, the information could flow many other ways, for example when you do choose to drive manually, and you jump a red light. The penalty/fine is immediately debited directly from your account, because when you decided to "drive" the vehicle you were required to confirm yourself as the driver of the vehicle. The vehicle then verified this to the necessary authorities. Your jumping the red light had immediate, verifiable consequences. Automated.

The 5G network will bring huge levels of automation into processes such as the driving example just provided. 5G will simply extend the wireless connectivity of so many people, things, and places. This generates Data and this will itself be part of a wider service. I see a time when a finance organisation requires Data to be streamed into them from the things they finance and fund. Why would a bank or other financial services organisation be interested? Well, if somebody contracts to look after an asset, this is a way that the finance organisation can be sure that the contractual "looking after" is happening, thus sustaining, or even increasing, the value of the asset. These same organisations may also carry some liability for missed safety checks. Basically, the Data was there; it will have been presented but fundamentally ignored. And there will be Data about the decision made to ignore the Data. A legal minefield is ahead when such things become common.

Summary

Some will be thinking that having a contract between a railway engine, a maintenance company, and a financial institution is madness; except it happens already. Technology will simply automate much of the contract and sustained verification of delivery against the terms of the contract across the life of the agreement. Why would you not do this if somebody is using a piece of equipment you fund? Why would you not have the right to know if it is being poorly maintained or being used beyond the specified limits of its design? In this case the Data becomes an asset in terms of supporting the quality and status of the liability that exists in the form of the funding or loan. 5G is the digital highway along and through which this information, this Data, will travel. It is the roads along which business will commute and meet. It is the byways along which AIs and Digital Twins will wander, engaging in dialogue and report about how they are doing, suggesting what can improve and all such things in-between. Critical to all of this will be the legal implications of this Data and the creation, use, distribution, and ultimately the destruction of this Data.

5G matters because it provides the means for the Digital economy to both grow and to thrive. 5G is a big step toward a very deep connection between the digital world and the real world that you and I inhabit. Legally, new opportunities are going to be created for contracts, agreements, MoUs, terms of use; all things that require clarity. The agreement and acceptance (or otherwise) of liability is going to be of significance. If your road sign provides bad information that my vehicle acts upon in good faith, and this bad information causes my vehicle to become damaged and damage other vehicles, who is liable? Who is responsible for the vehicle verifying the validity of the information broadcast by the road sign? I see interesting times ahead.

This chapter started by saying how the 2020s will be defined by Data; it already has been. This is beginning to have a profound impact upon the legal systems and professionals within these systems. Questions will abound, answers will be scarce. Do you need a digital twin to operate within the virtual world? What is a digital twin? Will AI replace human expertise? Should the legal profession use AI to enhance customer service and generate new revenue streams? It has been my hope that this chapter challenges thinking, provides examples showing the how, what, and who are leading the way. Overall, you should now have more questions than answers. But knowing the right question is the best place to start.

References

1. www.mckinsey.com/industries/retail/our-insights/how-retailers-can-keep-up-with-consumers
2. *Ibid.*
3. www.dell.com/en-us/blog/full-steam-ahead-railroads-with-ai-at-the-edge/
4. www.mckinsey.com/~/media/mckinsey/business%20functions/mckinsey%20digital/our%20insights/big%20data%20the%20next%20frontier%20for%20innovation/mgi_big_data_full_report.pdf
5. www.ofcom.org.uk/phones-telecoms-and-internet/advice-for-consumers/advice/what-is-5g

About Globe Law and Business

Globe Law and Business was established in 2005. From the very beginning, we set out to create law books which are sufficiently high level to be of real use to the experienced professional, yet still accessible and easy to navigate. Most of our authors are drawn from Magic Circle and other top commercial firms, both in the UK and internationally.

Our titles are carefully produced, with the utmost attention paid to editorial, design and production processes. We hope this results in high-quality publications that are easy to read, and a pleasure to own. Our titles are also available as ebooks, which are compatible with most desktop, laptop and tablet devices. In 2018 we expanded our portfolio to include journals and Special Reports, available both digitally and in hard copy format, and produced to the same high standards as our books.

In the spring of 2021, we were very pleased to announce the start of a new chapter for Globe Law and Business following the acquisition of law books under the imprint Ark Publishing. We are very much looking forward to working with our new Ark authors, many of whom are well known to us, to further developing the law firm management list, and to welcoming our new Ark customers.

We'd very much like to hear from you with your thoughts and ideas for improving what we offer. Please do feel free to email me at sian@globelawandbusiness.com with your views.

Sian O'Neill
Managing director
Globe Law and Business
www.globelawandbusiness.com

Related titles from Ark Publishing

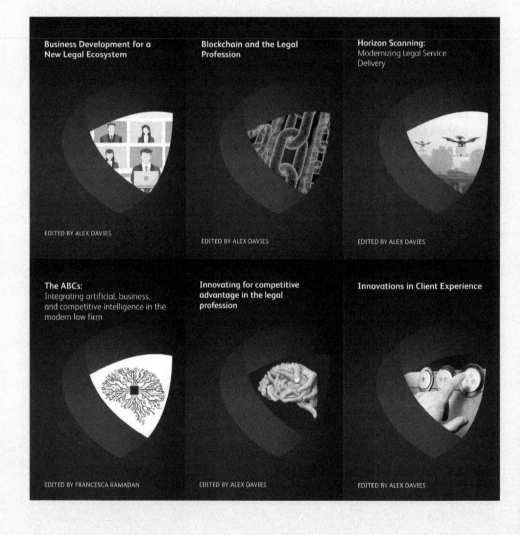

Go to **www.globelawandbusiness.com/ark**
for full details including free sample chapters